To Love, Honor, And Oh Boy!

30 Ways For Couples To Say
They're Wild About Each Other

Patty Mondore

CSS Publishing Company, Inc., Lima, Ohio

TO LOVE, HONOR, AND OH BOY!

Most scripture quotations are from the Holy Bible, New International Version. Copyright © 1973, 1978, 1984 International Bible Society. Used by permission of Zondervan Bible Publishers. All rights reserved.

Some scripture quotations are taken from the New Revised Standard Version of the Bible, copyright 1989 by the Division of Christian Education of the National Council of the Churches of Christ in the USA. Used by permission.

Some scripture quotations are from the Revised Standard Version of the Bible, copyrighted 1946, 1952 ©, 1971, 1973, by the Division of Christian Education of the National Council of the Churches of Christ in the USA. Used by permission.

Some scripture quotations are taken from the King James Version of the Bible, in the public domain.

Library of Congress Cataloging-in-Publication Data

Mondore, Patty.
    To love, honor, and oh boy! : 30 ways for couples to say they're wild about each other / Patty Mondore.
        p. cm.
    ISBN 0-7880-2467-1 (perfect bound : alk. paper)
    1. Marriage — Religious aspects — Christianity. 2. Love — Religious aspects — Christianity. I. Title.

    BV835.M647 2007
    248.8'44—dc22

                                                            2007024192

For more information about CSS Publishing Company resources, visit our website at www.csspub.com or email us at csr@csspub.com or call (800) 241-4056.

Cover design by Barbara Spencer and Nikki Nocera
ISBN-13: 978-0-7880-2467-2
ISBN-10: 0-7880-2467-1   PRINTED IN USA

I would like to dedicate To Love, Honor, And Oh Boy! *to the two couples most responsible for this book coming to be. Thank you, Mom and Dad, for pointing me to Christ. (Of course, giving birth to me was also a significant factor.) Thank you, Jessie, for raising Bob with a heart that was always open to the love of God. And though we have never met, I want to thank Irving C. Mondore for having been a father who was such a powerful role model to his son (the one I'm so wild about). I look forward to being able to tell him this myself when we meet some day, face to face. And of course, I dedicate this book to the man God gave me to love, honor, and, oh boy do I love Robert J. Mondore!*

Acknowledgments

Where do I begin? This book only exists because of the many dear couples, named, unnamed, and renamed, who were willing to share their beautiful stories with me and allow me, in turn, to share them with you. Most of them are very close friends (or, at least they were prior to this book coming out). Bless all of you for your willingness to let others laugh, cry, and most of all learn from the lessons you have experienced as married couples.

I would also like to especially acknowledge Wesley T. Runk, President of CSS Publishing, for his vision, his confidence in me, and for sharing a few stories of his own. I hope that *To Love, Honor, And Oh Boy!* lives up to your wildest expectations (and from what you've shared, that's pretty wild).

Finally, I know that every one of these couples would want to acknowledge, along with me, that it is our Lord and Savior, Jesus Christ, to whom we all owe our stories, our marriages, and, in fact, our very lives.

Table Of Contents

The Love Chapter
(1 Corinthians 13)

If I speak in the tongues of men and of angels, but have not love, I am only a resounding gong or a clanging cymbal. If I have the gift of prophecy and can fathom all mysteries and all knowledge, and if I have a faith that can move mountains, but have not love, I am nothing. If I give all I possess to the poor and surrender my body to the flames, but have not love, I gain nothing. Love is patient, love is kind. It does not envy, it does not boast, it is not proud. It is not rude, it is not self-seeking, it is not easily angered, it keeps no record of wrongs. Love does not delight in evil but rejoices with the truth. It always protects, always trusts, always hopes, always perseveres. Love never fails. But where there are prophecies, they will cease; where there are tongues, they will be stilled; where there is knowledge, it will pass away. For we know in part and we prophesy in part, but when perfection comes, the imperfect disappears. When I was a child, I talked like a child, I thought like a child, I reasoned like a child. When I became a man, I put childish ways behind me. Now we see but a poor reflection as in a mirror; then we shall see face to face. Now I know in part; then I shall know fully, even as I am fully known. And now these three remain: faith, hope and love. But the greatest of these is love.

Introduction

*And let us consider how we may spur one another on
toward love and good deeds.*   — Hebrews 10:24

I bet that at least a million books have been written on the subject of love and marriage. Okay, perhaps not quite a million, but lots! So, when I was asked to consider writing another one, my first thought was, "What's left to say that hasn't already been said?" and my second thought was, "Who, me?" Granted, God has blessed me and my dear husband, Bob, with a wonderful marriage. Granted, too, that we have had some unique ways of expressing our love to each other over the years. But I must admit I still felt a bit tentative (or, more precisely, completely overwhelmed) at the thought of offering insights and words of encouragement to other married couples. That is, until I got the idea of stealing ... er ... drawing from the wisdom (and lack thereof) of some of the other married couples I know. I also realized I could steal ... er ... borrow from the greatest source, in fact, the creator of marriage, himself. His book, the Bible, is of course the definitive source on love and how to express it. The author goes so far as to say that he, himself, *is* love ("God is love" 1 John 4:16). Sounds like a pretty good place, then, to find out how we, as married couples, can learn to love each other and express that love in new (and old) ways.

To Love, Honor, And Oh Boy! is a collection of thirty stories about real couples just like you and me (and my honey). Most of the couples are personal friends (or, at least they have been up until this book comes out). Others are couples whose stories are recorded for us in the scriptures. Through all of their examples (along with a few of my own), you'll discover how other couples have learned how (and how not) to demonstrate that they are wild about each other. In addition, I have paired each of their stories with one small piece of the "Love Chapter." Chapter 13 of Paul's letter to the believers at Corinth offers a concise yet practical explanation of what love is, and what it is not. I have broken the chapter down into

thirty bite-sized portions and have used some of those real-life stories of couples who have been blessed with strong marriages to illustrate each passage. At the end of each chapter, I leave you with one take-home point that you can begin to try out on each other. As I was working on this project and began to match the illustrations that I have with each of the verses, I found myself getting quite excited about how perfectly God's "Love Chapter" outlines what it takes to have the kind of marriage that glorifies the Lord. It also gives all of us married couples a very good reason to say, "Oh boy!"

Learning The Language

If I speak in the tongues of men and of angels, but have not love, I am only a resounding gong or a clanging cymbal. — 1 Corinthians 13:1

When people ask me at what point I first realized that Bob was the one for me, I usually tell them it was when I first saw him write in Greek on a napkin. Now I realize that conveying this particular epiphanic moment I had would probably not win Bob the award for the most romantic gesture ever performed by mankind (believe me, he's done plenty of those, too). But the Greek/napkin story is usually met with a rather blank stare. That's exactly what I'm hoping for. It gives me the chance to tell the whole story, once again.

I first met Bob at the Christian bookstore where we both worked. I ran the music department and he ran the store computer. He was also well known for being an expert in the area of cults. In fact, that is how we first got to know each other. I had just moved into a new home that was right across the street from a couple who were in a cult. I wanted to somehow be able to share my faith with them so I went to the resident expert to ask him how I could do that. Bob was more than willing to teach me what he knew about this particular group and to help prepare me for some of the issues that would no doubt come up if I tried to talk to them about the Lord. Since all of the music albums the store carried had to be entered into the computer before going on the shelves, they all needed to go through Bob before coming to my desk. He decided that this was the perfect opportunity for him, throughout the course of the day, to pass on little cult lessons to me. I would open the box of music and always find a note with a scripture verse or pointer dealing with

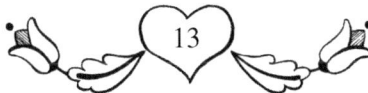

the deity of Christ, the Trinity, or some other doctrine critical to the faith. (Yes, I realize this doesn't sound very romantic just yet — hang in there with me.)

We had been doing this daily for several months when the invitation arrived. A couple from my neighborhood were getting married and they had invited everyone on the block to the reception. Being single, my invitation said, "and guest." I realized the couple I had been hoping to share my faith with would be there and I had what I considered to be a brilliant idea. I would ask Bob if he'd come with me and pretend to be my "date" (after all, we were just friends) in the hope that he might get to talk to the couple, himself. Bob was up for the challenge and we both began to pray that God would open the door for the two men to somehow meet and talk.

On the day of the reception I came to work and noticed that Bob was fighting off a cold and feeling a bit under the weather. By the end of the day, he was even running a fever. "You don't need to go," I said, doing my best to sound convincing. But Bob had promised he was going and that was all there was to it. He picked me up at my home and after praying one more time we headed to the party. When we arrived, we found there were hundreds of other guests. I wondered if we would even see the other couple, oh me of little faith. When it came time to be seated, we looked around for whatever place was available. Right in front of us, at one of the only tables with unclaimed seats, sat the couple. My heart began to pound. We walked over and I introduced my "date" to them and the two men ended up sitting right next to each other. I whispered a prayer of thanks and then continued to silently ask the Lord to give them the opportunity to talk about the Lord. But to my disappointment, there was a live band playing and one could barely hear the person next to them without having to shout. I just kept praying.

As the evening progressed, I looked over and noticed Bob and the man trying to have a conversation over the pounding rhythm of the band. I wondered what they were talking about. At one point a song came to an abrupt end and, caught off guard, the other man's voice broke the silence as he shouted something about Jesus, God,

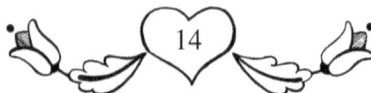

and Ho Theos (his wife looked mortified — I beamed). The music started back up and the intense conversation became increasingly animated. At one point Bob reached over, grabbed my napkin, and started jotting notes in Greek. I was in love!

Okay, so maybe I'm exaggerating my reaction just a bit. At least at that point in our relationship. However, what I saw in Bob that night was a man who loved God with all his heart, who had committed his life to studying God's word, and to sharing whatever he could (even Greek on napkins) to help others find God, as well. I may not have realized it at the time (or maybe I did — I'll never tell), but what I saw in him was everything I could ever want in a husband.

It wasn't until several months later that some of that love ended up being expressed toward each other. The little lessons continued to arrive each day in my box of music. Then, one day, I opened the box, took out the note, and instead of a scripture on the deity of Christ it simply said, "Hey, baby!" I immediately called my best friend and asked her if she knew what this meant (it clearly wasn't Greek). Her initial reaction was that it was possible we were moving away from cult studies and on to new areas of mutual interest. She was right.

Now, perhaps you are still wondering what Greek on napkins has to do with expressions of love. There are plenty of people who know scriptures, and even Greek. And of those who don't, many others know how to lavish the object of their attentions with romantic words and charming platitudes. The Love Chapter begins with an admonition that one could loosely paraphrase to read, "talk is cheap but love is action." It was a true expression of love for Bob, fever and all, to go somewhere with a bunch of strangers (he hates parties, by the way) on the remote chance that he could share Christ's love with someone trapped in a cult. Even the time he had invested in learning Greek was primarily to help others come to know the God of love. Bob was putting his love for others into action fulfilling God's call to each of us: "Dear children, let us not love with words or tongue but with actions and in truth" (1 John

3:18). Bob spoke with the tongues of Greeks that night at the reception and though I still don't understand a word of Greek (except baklava), I do know the language of love when I hear it. Bob's life is an expression of that love. That's why I fell in love with him. Though, I must admit the "Hey, baby" didn't hurt either.

Love puts its thoughts into action.

Eating Her Words

If I have the gift of prophecy and can fathom all mysteries and all knowledge, and if I have a faith that can move mountains, but have not love, I am nothing.
— 1 Corinthians 13:2

Oh, to be able to capture and hang on to some of those initial joys of our newlywed years. We can all remember some of our faltering first steps as married couples and how we wanted everything to be extra special. We went out of our way to lavish each other with tender acts of kindness — bouquets of flowers, favorite meals, love notes, greeting each other at the end of the day with a big kiss, and most of all, making our beloved feel like the most special person in the world. One of the secrets to a happy marriage is in hanging on to some of those early expressions of love throughout our marriage. Before Bob and I got married, I had read that the patterns a couple set in their first year of marriage will often remain for the rest of their lives. So, I was determined (and Bob was more than willing to humor me) to set some good ones.

From the day we went down the aisle, whenever we walked anywhere together I took hold of Bob's arm. At eighteen years and counting we still walk arm-in-arm without even thinking about it. In fact, it is so ingrained in me that if I take a walk with a girlfriend I have to catch myself to not automatically reach for her arm. Even though Bob and I both work, I am almost always home before he is. From the beginning I made a point to stop whatever I am doing (and I am always doing something), and run to the door to greet him with a big kiss when he gets home. If, for some reason, he happens to get home before I do, he does the same to me. These are

just a few of the little habits we have developed. True to what I read, the patterns we set early in our marriages do tend to stick for life, so, be creative. Like my friend, Tracey, and her husband, Phil.

Tracey and Phil hadn't meant to set a pattern that would last for life but once they started it, you might say it started to feed on itself. It began on their wedding day (May 14). Most people have a toast at their reception. Tracey and Phil were no exception, other than what they decided to use to make their toast. As an admitted, self-professing chocoholic, Tracey came up with the idea of having a chocolate toast. They bought $200 worth of Godiva Raspberry Truffles, passed them out to everyone at the reception, and at the set time each of the guests "clinked" truffles and toasted the bride and groom. Ever since then, on the fourteenth day of every month, they have commemorated the date by clinking (and of course eating) a Godiva raspberry truffle. When Godiva discontinued that truffle, not to be deterred, they made a smooth transition to the Lindt brand (or, Tracey-the-gourmet-chef has even been known to buy fresh raspberries and dip them in chocolate, herself). In twelve years, they have never missed a month.

Bob's parents had a similar tradition of their own, almost fifty years before Tracey and Phil. Irving and Jessie were married on September 19, 1948, at 4 p.m. in a tiny Dutch Reformed church in Kingston, New York. After the first month, on the nineteenth of every month at exactly (well, as close as possible) 4 p.m., Irving would take Jessie to Robert's Diner for apple pie with ice cream (that was the special treat they had on their honeymoon). They kept that tradition going right up until the kids started coming (perhaps that explains, in part, Bob's attraction to pie à la mode).

Yes, those first years together are the perfect time to set some wonderful traditions that will help keep the romance in your marriage. Of course, there are other aspects of newly wedded bliss that one can only hope time and knowledge will heal. Young love combined with perhaps a little too much creativity can sometimes lead to some potentially unappetizing expressions of affection. Such is the lesson we can learn from Rex and Cheryl. At the time, this young couple was in their fifth or sixth year of marriage. Cheryl

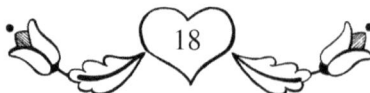

was already in the habit of making lunch for Rex before he left for work each day. But one day, to add a little variety to his lunch, Cheryl decided to slip a romantic note, not just in the bag, but right inside his sandwich. She hadn't really given much thought to the fact that laying there next to the meat, the paper might get a little wilty. When Rex got home that evening and failed to mention her tender expression of love, she asked him about it. When she told him she had put a love note in his sandwich he had no idea what she was talking about. It was only then that they both realized the paper had absorbed so much moisture from the meat that he had eaten the whole sandwich, love note, and all. After getting over the initial trauma of pondering the long-term effects of ingested paper and ink, they laughed about the whole incident for years to come. Nevertheless, after that, Cheryl decided it would be more practical to put her love notes on the fruit, instead. Especially the oranges and bananas. That way she could be sure he would see her message rather than eat it.

There are several observations one could make about this particular tradition. First, it gives a whole new meaning to the concept of taking in knowledge. In fact, it sort of reminds me of a dialogue God had with Ezekiel where he said, " 'Son of man, eat what you find; eat this scroll, and go, speak to the house of Israel.' So I opened my mouth, and he fed me this scroll. He said to me, 'Son of man, feed your stomach and fill your body with this scroll which I am giving you.' Then I ate it, and it was sweet as honey in my mouth" (Ezekiel 3:1-3). Cheryl's sweet love note fed Rex's stomach, too. Though, in their case, it was probably more due to the companion products in the sandwich, than to the note itself.

Second, and more importantly, one could conclude that even paper tastes good when prepared by the hands of one's beloved. I think Solomon had this same thought in mind when he wrote, "Better a meal of vegetables where there is love than a fattened calf with hatred" (Proverbs 15:17). One could be the most highly trained chef in the world but not be able to prepare a meal as tasty as a simple sandwich served with love. Over the years we will (hopefully) learn to grow beyond some of those silly newlywed

love-goofs. We will get to know each other (and a little more about making paper-free sandwiches). But hopefully, with that knowledge, we will never grow beyond the habit and desire to continually seek to express our love in new and creative ways. As the Love Chapter reminds us, "If I have ... all knowledge ... but have not love, I am nothing." So keep holding hands, sharing chocolates or pie à la mode, making sandwiches, or even try a new recipe for passing on romantic messages and words of endearment to each other. The words themselves may be forgotten (or even eaten, on occasion), but our continued expressions of love will last through eternity.

**Love sets traditions yet keeps coming up
with new ways to express itself.**

Gazelles And Pantyhose

*If I give all I possess to the poor and surrender my body
to the flames, but have not love, I gain nothing.*
— 1 Corinthians 13:3

It was women's night out. A bunch of us decided to go out for coffee one weekday evening. Most of us were still single, but a few of the women were on loan from their husbands and kids.

Diane (not her real name) was a young pastor's wife. We were delighted we could get her to come and join us. She was always a lot of fun and we single girls were always looking for pointers from someone who had "landed" a pastor for a husband. Carl (not her husband's real name) stayed home with the baby for the night. The main reason I'm protecting Carl and Diane's identities is that I would hate to see the story we managed to get out of Diane that night (it took several cups of coffee and an ice cream sundae to break her down) get into the hands of the *National Enquirer* or the *Globe* (not to mention the paparazzi). Because this particular story is just plain hot!

Diane was telling us about their first few years as a married couple. They had met in college and were married at the end of their senior year. That is also when Carl felt the call to go into the ministry. For a young couple just out of college with debts to pay, the prospect of jumping right into seminary seemed daunting to say the least. But they decided that this is what the Lord was leading them to do and, that being the case, God would somehow provide for them. Carl was accepted into school and started classes that same year. Diane got a full-time job and things were looking pretty good until, two months into the first semester, they discovered they were soon to become parents. Should he quit school and

get a job so Diane could stay home with the baby? After seeking God once again, they both agreed Carl should stay in school, Diane would stay home and raise their child, and they would continue to trust God to meet their financial needs. Carl got a fairly good paying part-time job working the night shift in a bakery. But, needless to say, things were going to be tight for a while, and between school, work, and a newborn baby, Carl and Diane were both as stretched, physically and emotionally, as any young couple could be. Yet, they still believed they were right where God wanted them to be. And somehow their bills always ended up being paid.

Still, there was most certainly no room for luxuries or extras. When their second anniversary was approaching, and Diane wanted to do something extra special for her overworked, underpaid sweetheart, she had no idea what to do. They didn't even have the money to go out for a nice dinner. She did find some friends willing to take the baby for the evening so they could at least spend a quiet evening together at home. She had longingly looked through some of the expensive lingerie catalogs wishing she could splurge and buy some cute, skimpy nightgown for their romantic evening together. But, alas, that wasn't going to happen. However, as she was looking at those catalogs, Diane came up with an alternative plan.

Diane knew how to sew fairly well. She decided she would make her own skimpy nighty. But, once again, money was an issue. Could she even afford the fabric it would require? As she was considering her options, she looked over on the clothesline and saw several pairs of pantyhose drying on the line. But while some might have seen nothing more than wet stockings, visions of Frederick's of Hollywood were suddenly dancing in Diane's eyes.

A few weeks later when the anniversary arrived, Diane was ready. The bigger question was, *Would Carl be ready for what he was about to experience?* Carl came home from school and immediately headed back out the door for his night shift. "I'll make it up to you, honey," he said, clearly feeling bad that he couldn't be with her on the eve of their anniversary. "We'll do something special this weekend, I promise." Diane assured him that she understood. "Don't worry about it, Carl. I'll have a special treat for you when

you get home tonight." No doubt, visions of Diane's homemade chocolate cake were dancing through Carl's head as he worked that evening. The minute his shift was over he punched out, jumped in the car, and ... well, got home a little quicker than usual.

He opened the door expecting to find Diane there waiting for him. Instead, he came in to a pitch dark room. "I'm home, honey," he shouted as he flipped on the light switch. There, standing just across the room, stood Diane wearing, well, it's kind of hard to describe, but "not much" would be the closest description. Diane had taken a few pairs of pantyhose (it didn't take very many) and designed a lovely little see-through negligee that she was now modeling for her beloved. Carl's first response, or at least the first words he could get out of his mouth after several moments of stunned silence, was, "Whoa!" Needless to say, Carl completely forgot about chocolate cake. In fact, I'm pretty sure they decided to skip dinner altogether.

People have accused Christians of having boring, puritanical, uptight, joyless marriages (not to mention their love lives). That certainly wasn't ever God's intent. Listen to how the Bible describes the marriage relationship:

Take me away with you — let us hurry! Let the king bring me into his chambers. — Song of Solomon 1:4

How delightful is your love, my sister, my bride! How much more pleasing is your love than wine, and the fragrance of your perfume than any spice!
— Song of Solomon 4:10

I am my lover's and my lover is mine; he browses among the lilies. — Song of Solomon 6:3

How beautiful you are and how pleasing, O love, with your delights! — Song of Solomon 7:6

I belong to my lover, and his desire is for me.
— Song of Solomon 7:10

If you need any more proof, just read the Song of Solomon. These are not the words describing a boring relationship. These are passionate expressions of an all-consuming physical/emotional/spiritual love that only a husband and wife can share. In fact, God has used this perfect union to describe the kind of intimate relationship he longs to have with his bride, the church.

It is worth noting that Carl didn't care that Diane's negligee didn't come from an expensive department store. In fact, had she had all the money in the world to splurge for their romantic evening, she couldn't have delighted him any more than she did with that simple pair of pantyhose. Solomon concurs: "Many waters cannot quench love; rivers cannot wash it away. If one were to give all the wealth of his house for love, it would be utterly scorned" (Song of Solomon 8:7).

No, it doesn't take a lot of money for a couple to enjoy a rich and exciting love life. Diane gave Carl the gift that mattered the most — wrapped in the thinnest veneer of nylon, she gave her beloved her body and her heart. All the money in the world can't buy any better gift than in giving ourselves to each other in love. And nothing could be more pure and beautiful.

Love gives itself, body, soul, and spirit, to its beloved.

Lost On The Way To A Man's Heart

Love ... is patient.   — 1 Corinthians 13:4a

It was a well-established fact, long before Bob said, "I do" that he was marrying someone who, when it comes to survival skills in the kitchen would have had to honestly answer, "I don't." In other words, to phrase it as an understatement, I am not a very good cook. If my warnings hadn't been enough, my friends had been more than willing to fill in all of the gory details about my functionality (or lack thereof) in the domestic arts — cooking being at the top (or, shall we say the bottom) of the list. Truth be told, there was almost a degree of pride in my bold declaration that I can't cook (not to mention all the potluck suppers I got out of having to contribute to). Lest you think I am exaggerating, it only took a few Mondore holiday gatherings for my new family to figure out I was the one they should assign either napkins or paper plates as my dish to pass (I think I locked it in once and for all, the year I took the La Choy casserole).

Still, true love has a way of bringing the best out of even the most committed anti-domestic. So, when I overheard Bob telling his mom how much he had always loved cherry squares as a little boy, something welled up inside me that apparently had been lying dormant. I wanted to make Bob his cherry squares. So, unbeknownst to Bob, I called his mom up and asked her for the recipe. I have to admit she did her best to hide her shock and concern (especially considering it had only been a few months since the La Choy episode), as she carefully (perhaps a little too carefully) read the ingredients and instructions to me over the phone. "Yes, I can do this!" I said to myself and was out the door with my shopping list in hand.

The ingredients seemed harmless enough — butter, sugar, eggs, flour, nuts, vanilla, and cherry pie filling (in a can, no less — what could possibly go wrong?). I mixed the stuff I was supposed to mix (butter, eggs, and sugar) and started to add the other ingredients (vanilla, flour, and ... *chopped* nuts?). Hmm. I had somehow missed the chopped part. Well, not to worry. I would just chop the nuts myself. That would make my cherry squares even more homemade. Though, just how does one go about chopping nuts? And how chopped is chopped? Somehow, all those instructions I had been given suddenly seemed utterly inadequate. But never having been one to admit defeat, I started to dig through the kitchen drawers and check out some of the many gizmos people had given us for wedding presents (most still in their original packages). When I found the grater I realized my search was over. Chopped — grated — what's the difference?

The whole process was admittedly a little bit cumbersome. I picked up a handful of nuts at a time and ran them over the grater into the bowl below. It was slow work but that's what love's all about, right? In a not-too-horribly-long time, I had just about a full cup of some fine looking chopped nuts. As I was brushing off my hands (it's a dirty job, you know), to my horror I suddenly noticed that some of the bandage that had been covering a cut on my finger was ... well, missing. And below that, some of my finger was missing. Without even realizing it, I had added a little bit of grated bandage and finger into the mix. Talk about putting yourself into your work.

I paused (only for less than a second or two — honest!), to consider what my options were. I must admit it did go through my mind that this could give a whole new meaning to the term, "finger food." But, of course, I immediately dumped the whole bowl of my hard labors (and finger) in the trash and started over, this time being much more careful to be sure I remained intact in the process. From that point on, things actually went smoothly and it wasn't long before I was pulling a dish of bubbling hot cherry squares out of the oven. I can't tell you how much joy it gave me to be able to

present my husband with his favorite homemade dessert. Any reservations Bob may have had in knowing it had been handmade by his boastfully inept kitchen manager, he kept completely to himself. The only response I saw was the love and appreciation he lavished on me. Knowing my aversion to cooking-related issues, he was touched all the more by my loving presentation and was determined to make sure I knew he was delighted by the expression of love it represented.

The point of my retelling of this particular kitchen adventure is that if you ever invite Bob and me to your potluck, you might seriously consider asking me to bring the paper plates. But more importantly, I hope you see that the home, even the home of a culinary wannabe, can and should be a place where we are continually able to try out new recipes for love. And the only way that can happen is if we live in a home where there is patience when we don't get things quite right. Or even when we totally mess up.

Bob ate those cherry squares (albeit cautiously at first) and claims to this day that they were delicious. Yet, I know for a fact that, even if they weren't, Bob would never have said a negative or hurtful word. For someone who married a woman who is admittedly culinarily challenged, few wives have received any more appreciation than I have for whatever I put on the table, in whatever condition it arrives. And I am well aware that some of the conditions have been well below substandard. Oh, sure, there have been a few times (okay, plenty of times) when Bob was simply unable to eat something I prepared (we won't go into my shoe leather steak story). Even then, his response was gracious. My feelings were more important to him than to chew me out over a steak he couldn't chew. And my response — actually anyone's response — is to want to do whatever I can to please him. I think Solomon addressed it quite well when he wrote: "A man's wisdom gives him patience; it is to his glory to overlook an offense" (Proverbs 19:11). Spouses are blessed and God is glorified when we are able to lovingly look past each other's shortcomings.

I am thankful that the way to my man's heart wasn't through his stomach. Bob is, first and foremost, committed to showing the

kind of love Paul challenged all of us to exemplify toward one another: "Therefore, as God's chosen people, holy and dearly loved, clothe yourselves with compassion, kindness, humility, gentleness, and patience. Bear with each other and forgive whatever grievances you may have against one another. Forgive as the Lord forgave you. And over all these virtues put on love, which binds them all together in perfect unity" (Colossians 3:12-14).

Bob's not perfect (we'd have been incompatible if he was), but because he has tried to make our home a place of acceptance and love, he has earned himself a lifetime supply of homemade cherry squares (they're not perfect either, but definitely made with a lot of love).

Love looks past each other's weaknesses.

An In-Tents Love

Love is kind.   — 1 Corinthians 13:4b

We don't know too much about them. But the few times they are mentioned in the scriptures reveal enough for us to know they had a very strong marriage — strong enough that all of us married couples could learn from their example. The first time we encounter Priscilla and Aquila is right along with Paul when he first arrived in Corinth. Paul was on one of his missionary journeys and was following Christ's mandate to "go into all the world" and to "make disciples of all the nations." Jesus had given his disciples a clear plan to follow as they went saying, "And whatever city or village you enter, inquire who is worthy in it, and stay at his house until you leave that city. As you enter the house, give it your greeting. If the house is worthy, give it your blessing of peace" (Matthew 10:11-13). After his adventures in Athens, Paul was probably hoping to find a little respite in the home of some fellow believers. He found that and more when the Lord led him to Priscilla and Aquila.

Aquila, a Jew who was a native of Pontus, had only recently arrived in Corinth himself. He and his wife, Priscilla, had been forced to flee Rome after all Jews were expelled by the emperor Claudius. We aren't told whether Aquila and Priscilla were already Christians before meeting Paul, or whether they came to Christ through his preaching, but soon after he arrived Paul went to see them, "and because he was a tentmaker as they were, he stayed and worked with them" (Acts 18:3). Paul moved in with Aquila and Priscilla and from that time on he referred to them as his faithful

coworkers. In fact, when he finished his work in Corinth and moved on to his next mission, he took Priscilla and Aquila with him. We read, "Paul stayed on in Corinth for some time. Then he left the brothers and sailed for Syria, accompanied by Priscilla and Aquila ... They arrived at Ephesus ..." (Acts 18:18-19).

The next time this dynamic couple is mentioned, we get a glimpse of the kind of quiet but effective ministry they shared. While they were working with Paul in Ephesus, "... a Jew named Apollos, a native of Alexandria, came to Ephesus. He was a learned man, with a thorough knowledge of the scriptures. He had been instructed in the way of the Lord, and he spoke with great fervor and taught about Jesus accurately, though he knew only the baptism of John. He began to speak boldly in the synagogue. When Priscilla and Aquila heard him, they invited him to their home and explained to him the way of God more adequately" (Acts 18:24-26).

Rather than publicly confronting Apollos about his lack of knowledge, this godly couple quietly pulled him aside and shared Christ with him. The result of their faithful witness was phenomenal. Apollos, now grounded in the truth, went forth and led many to Christ with his bold witness. We read, "When Apollos wanted to go to Achaia, the brothers encouraged him and wrote to the disciples there to welcome him. On arriving, he was a great help to those who by grace had believed. For he vigorously refuted the Jews in public debate, proving from the scriptures that Jesus was the Christ" (Acts 18:27-28). At some point, Priscilla and Aquila started a house church of their own. In his letter to the church at Corinth Paul wrote, "The churches in the province of Asia send you greetings. Aquila and Priscilla greet you warmly in the Lord, and so does the church that meets at their house" (1 Corinthians 16:19).

The last mention of Priscilla and Aquila is in Paul's letter to the church at Rome. He ends by sending the following personal message to his beloved friends: "Greet Priscilla and Aquila, my fellow workers in Christ Jesus. They risked their lives for me. Not only I but all the churches of the Gentiles are grateful to them" (Romans 16:3-4). The word Paul uses for "fellow workers" in the

Greek is *synergoi*. One doesn't have to know much Greek (I don't know any) to see that this is where we get the word "synergy." Synergy is defined as "the working together of two or more people, organizations, or things, especially when the result is greater than the sum of their individual effects or capabilities." Priscilla and Aquila worked synergistically with Paul to spread the gospel and believed strongly enough in what they were doing that they were willing, as a couple, to die for it.

Note that there is not a single mention of either Priscilla or Aquila without the other. Every time their names appear in the scriptures, they are together serving the Lord as colaborers or in synergy with each other. What a beautiful model they make for every Christian couple — to work together as *one* serving the Lord. And when, as couples, we work together with him, the results are certain to far exceed anything we could accomplish on our own. One other interesting note about Priscilla and Aquila is that, like Paul, they were tentmakers by trade. It is no doubt due to the three of them that the term "tentmaker" has come to take on the meaning that it has today. It is an expression used to describe missionaries who go into a foreign country to share Christ while supporting themselves through their own trade (or secular employment). This definition perfectly fits Priscilla and Aquila who, as I mentioned earlier, were foreigners and tentmakers in Corinth. Together with Paul, they were the first official tentmakers using the modern definition.

There is something else about them being tentmakers that makes Priscilla and Aquila's life work particularly appropriate. As anyone who has ever gone camping could attest to, tents are nothing more than temporary dwellings. As believers it is easy to see the analogy of living in a tent and of our temporary physical lives here on earth. Paul, himself, used this illustration in his writings saying, "For we know that if the earthly tent we live in is destroyed, we have a building from God, a house not made with hands, eternal in the heavens. Here indeed we groan, and long to put on our heavenly dwelling, so that by putting it on we may not be found naked. For while we are still in this tent, we sigh with anxiety; not that we

would be unclothed, but that we would be further clothed, so that what is mortal may be swallowed up by life" (2 Corinthians 5:1-4 RSV).

Abraham and Sarah, two lifelong tent dwellers themselves, also understood the temporariness of this life. We read, "By faith Abraham obeyed when he was called to go out to a place which he was to receive as an inheritance; and he went out, not knowing where he was to go. By faith he sojourned in the land of promise, as in a foreign land, living in tents with Isaac and Jacob, heirs with him of the same promise. For he looked forward to the city which has foundations, whose builder and maker is God" (Hebrews 11:8-10 RSV).

Priscilla and Aquila did not consider this world their permanent dwelling place either. That is why they were willing to expend all of their time, energy, money, and even risk their very lives together as a husband and wife, for the city whose builder and maker is God.

**Love works together as a team
that can be used mightily by God.**

Plain And Simple

It does not envy. — 1 Corinthians 13:4c

He fell from a 34-foot silo. No one expected he would live.
But he did. He was taken, in critical condition, to the hospital where
I work. Some friends of mine contacted me to see if I could find
out how he was doing, since none of his family had phones. That's
because Jake Stoltzfus and his wife, Lydia* are Amish. At first I
hesitated. Would they be offended that I was asking? Would they
rather be left alone at such a time of crisis? I felt that familiar nudge
urging me to get involved so, despite my reservations, I headed to
the critical care area praying as I went.

As I walked past the waiting room, I saw about a dozen Amish
people. I realized I could just ask his wife how he was doing and
then report back to my friends and be done with it. When I walked
into the room everyone looked up at me. "Is Mrs. Stoltzfus here?"
I asked. About half of the hands in the room went up. The other
half were men. Okay, that didn't work. I tried again. I let them
know I was a friend of one of their neighbors and I was looking for
Jake's wife. Several of the women, all wearing white caps and dark
dresses, came over and warmly greeted me and filled me in. Lydia
was down the hall with her husband, who was on life support and
in critical condition. He had broken his back in several places and
hit his head, and at that point it was too early to tell if he was going
to make it. The women suggested that I go down and pass on my
friends' greetings to Lydia for myself. I was horrified. "Oh no, I
couldn't do that. She's going through so much, and she wouldn't
know who I am and...." I felt myself gently being escorted down
the hall. I looked in the room and saw a young woman and three

young children standing at an unconscious Jake's bedside. A weary-looking Lydia looked up and caught my eye. My heart melted. She signaled for me to come into the room. I blurted out how very sorry I was and to please let me know if there was anything I could do to help. With tears in her eyes she thanked me. Thus began my friendship with Lydia.

Clearly, it wasn't time for Jake to leave his wife and eight children because over the next few days the changes could almost be described as miraculous. Jake's condition stabilized and he was taken off all life support. It appeared that he was going to be permanently paralyzed from waist down, but all that mattered to Lydia was that Jake would be coming home. Just over a week after entering the hospital, Jake was "promoted" to the rehab unit where he would spend the next six weeks learning life from the perspective of a wheelchair. I came to visit almost every day. Though Lydia enjoyed telling me about the Amish way of life, most of what I learned simply came from being with them and all of the family and friends who were constantly visiting throughout their hospital stay. What impressed me most about the Amish people is their sense of community. From the time he arrived, until the time he left, there were always at least two and sometimes up to a dozen members of the community there supporting him and his wife. I was deeply touched at how the Amish people lovingly provide for one another. Without their even asking, it was understood that someone would take care of the Stoltzfus' children back home, tend to their livestock, their garden, and other household needs. As soon as they heard Jake would be coming home in a wheelchair, the men built ramps on their house to make it accessible to him.

I also discovered their sense of humor. I was telling them about how some of the sick children would dress up on Halloween and be taken around the hospital to go trick-or-treating. Jake thought about that for a moment and then wondered, out loud, if he followed along in his wheelchair whether people might think he was dressed up as an Amish man and give him chocolate. One of his Amish friends volunteered to push him around for 50% of the profits. Lydia just rolled her eyes. I could see she'd been through this

before and that the two of them could easily get themselves into all kinds of fun-loving trouble if left unattended.

As for Lydia and Jake, it was obvious that they loved each other deeply. They also had a quiet and unspoken understanding between them. No matter what Lydia doing, or who she was talking to, she was constantly aware of Jake's every move and anticipated his needs. Having been married for over fourteen years, she seemed to know, without him even speaking, what he was thinking and what she could do to help. And Jake had a quiet confidence in his wife. Whenever she gently asked him to do something (or not to), his response was immediate. Through the entire ordeal, I watched Lydia calmly face each terrifying moment and each new complication with a quiet but steady faith. And that inner strength made her beautiful, despite her plain Amish dress. She seemed to exemplify Peter's admonition to all us women: "Your beauty should not come from outward adornment, such as braided hair and the wearing of gold jewelry and fine clothes. Instead, it should be that of your inner self, the unfading beauty of a gentle and quiet spirit, which is of great worth in God's sight. For this is the way the holy women of the past who put their hope in God used to make themselves beautiful" (1 Peter 3:3-5).

Like many of the Amish who have chosen this austere lifestyle of hard work and few luxuries, Lydia and Jake had faced tragedy, loss, and financial difficulties before, and God had always brought them through. They could honesty say, along with Paul, "I have learned the secret of being content in any and every situation, whether well fed or hungry, whether living in plenty or in want. I can do everything through him who gives me strength" (Philippians 4:12-13). With their confidence in him, they would face this new challenge together. Lydia would do whatever she could to provide for her family, and she trusted God to take care of the rest. They had gotten married and assumed a lifetime of caring for each other no matter what they might face. And they do so with a simple, quiet trust in God.

Lydia and Jake have now returned home. Life will be quite different for them. It will not be easy. This once strong, young man

who held down two jobs to make ends meet will no longer be farming the land or climbing silos. In other ways, however, life will be much the same. They will continue to lead their quiet, hard working lives together, trusting in God to provide for their needs. And I know he will. As James put it, "Listen, my dear brothers: Has not God chosen those who are poor in the eyes of the world to be rich in faith and to inherit the kingdom he promised those who love him?" (James 2:5). By the only standard that really matters, Lydia and Jake are downright rich. And if you ask them, they wouldn't want it any other way.

**Love doesn't need great wealth
or earthly possessions to be truly rich.**

---

* These are not their real names. The Amish are very humble people and out of respect for their privacy, I have given them new Amish names.

Many Mansions

It does not boast. — 1 Corinthians 13:4d

One of the lines in the traditional wedding vows is, "For richer or for poorer." My Amish friends are living proof that a marriage can remain strong, and even flourish, with only the barest necessities of life. But what about the "for richer" part? We've all seen the divorce stories of the rich and famous. Wealth can put a strain on marriages. Or, it can make them stronger. It's all a matter of priorities. I can think of at least one couple who lived this out.

When my parents suggested we visit a Sunday church service that meets in a castle, I had no interest in going. Well, that's not entirely true. I thought it would be neat to visit a real castle, located on an island in the Thousand Islands. What I had no interest in was the kind of "church service" I assumed someone with that kind of ostentatious wealth would give. I was quickly proven wrong. We arrived at as magnificent a castle as I had ever seen. We, along with the other guests, were escorted to the large chapel where we were greeted by the castle owners, Drs. Harold and Eloise Martin. At the beginning of the service, it was admittedly hard to pay attention to the message, being captivated by the stunningly beautiful surroundings. But it didn't take long to realize we were hearing a very straightforward gospel message. At one point, an elegantly dressed Eloise rose, at her husband's request, and sang one of the beautiful old hymns for us. The Martins were an older couple yet their love for each other was obvious. Eloise returned to her seat and Harold ended the service by quoting John 3:16 — "For God so loved the world that he gave his one and only Son, that whoever believes in him shall not perish but have eternal life" — and asking

if anyone in the room did not know Jesus as their personal Savior. He then ended with prayer. I bowed my head and asked the Lord to forgive me for judging the Martins based on all of their perceived wealth.

Harold and Eloise first met at Moody Bible College where they were both students. Young Harold was studying in his room one night with the campus radio station playing in the background. Suddenly (as he tells the story), he was so taken with the voice of the woman singing on the radio that he ran over to the studio and got his first glimpse of Eloise as she sang live, on the air. He knew right then and there that she was the one for him. When he introduced himself to her, hoping he could bypass the courtship stuff and get right to the proposal, he quickly found out she hadn't had the same immediate revelation. However, it wasn't long before she did, and their good friend, George Beverly Shea, sang at their wedding.

I was talking with Eloise one day long before I met Bob and asked her what it was like to be married to the man of her dreams. I was somewhat surprised by her response. She told me that when she first married Harold she had idolized him. Her whole life, emotions, and well-being revolved around him. She went through a real struggle with this early in their marriage and came to realize that she needed to put the Lord first, and find her completeness and satisfaction in him. When she was able to let him be the ultimate source of her happiness and strength, she was free to truly love her husband. When Eloise released her husband to him, the Lord gave her the kind of marriage she had always dreamed of. He also began to open up opportunities for the two of them to minister to others beyond anything they could have dreamed of. Together, they spent their lives serving the Lord and touching lives all over the world (including in a castle), with the love of Christ.

We started going to Jorstadt regularly after that first service. As I got to know the Martins better I discovered that despite all their apparent wealth, they had purchased the castle for an unbelievably low price. They had a Christian ministry in nearby Canada. When they heard that the castle had gone on the market, they made

a ridiculously low offer for it. When the owners accepted the offer, the Martins could only conclude that God was giving it to them as yet another opportunity to serve him. For the next thirty years, Jorstadt Castle became a Christian retreat center for missionaries, churches, youth, and a Sunday morning church service. That, of course, required money. Upkeep of the castle, alone, was astronomical. So, while some couples their age were spending their retirement years sitting on a beach in Florida, the Martins spent their winters working, and working hard, to keep their castle ministry running. When asked if it was worth it all, Eloise answered, "If even one person comes to know the Lord here, one soul is far more valuable than the cost of a castle and a little hard work."

Over the years, several groups from my church went to the castle for "work weekends" doing whatever we could to help the Martins out. And believe me, there was plenty to do. But the memories we left with weren't of the hard work but rather of the Martins, themselves. After dinner, we would all sit together with the Martins in the loggia and just listen as they shared their stories with us, sometimes into the wee hours of the morning. They told us about some of the 72 countries where Harold had shared the gospel, and Eloise's home for unwed mothers, and the stories of many individuals the Lord had allowed them to lead to Christ through the colabors of their love.

On one occasion, we finally realized it was only a matter of hours until we all had to get up for church. When Harold gave his message the next morning, he told the congregation that when he woke up, as he so often did, he asked Eloise, "What shall I preach on today? And she told me the same thing she does every Sunday. Preach on love, dear. You can't ever tell them too many times about the love of God." And, as he always did, Harold preached on the love of God, ending once again with John 3:16.

The Martins never boasted about any of their accomplishments, education (they both had doctorates), or worldly possessions (including their castle). They knew that all they had belonged to God. They poured everything they had — their time, their money, their energy — into serving the Lord together. When they passed away,

they didn't leave a large fortune behind. (Anyone want to make an offer on a used castle?) Nevertheless, they spent their lives making wise investments. As the scriptures put it, "Command those who are rich in this present world not to be arrogant nor to put their hope in wealth, which is so uncertain, but to put their hope in God, who richly provides us with everything for our enjoyment. Command them to do good, to be rich in good deeds, and to be generous and willing to share. In this way, they will lay up treasure for themselves as a firm foundation for the coming age, so that they may take hold of the life that is truly life" (1 Timothy 6:17-19). Today, Harold and Eloise Martin are finally getting to enjoy some of those retirement benefits.

Love gives all it has to God and then overflows to others.

Best Friends

It is not proud.   — 1 Corinthians 13:4e

It was what some might consider a rather unlikely marital success story, from the very beginning — a couple of teenagers, both from troubled homes, getting married right out of high school. Oh, and they lived in a trailer park. Talk about humble beginnings. In fact, even the way they met was anything but promising. It started as a joke. They were juniors in high school and rode the same bus to their BOCES class. Gail and her girlfriends sat together chattering and laughing all the way to class. Chip, on the other hand, sat by himself and never spoke a word to anyone. One of Gail's friends thought it would be funny to try to match the loudest girl on the bus (Gail) with the quietest boy (Chip). So, unbeknownst to either of them, Gail's friend secretly stuck a note in Chip's pocket that said, "I want go to the prom with you" with Gail's name and phone number. It wasn't Chip who found the note. When his mom was doing the laundry she pulled it out of his pocket and was curious enough (and perhaps thrilled to think her introverted son actually had a girlfriend), to call the number on the note. When Gail's dad answered, the two of them decided their kids would be perfect for each other, and went ahead and arranged the date.

I'm not sure why either of them agreed to it, but somehow Gail ended up going to the prom with Chip. And somewhere along the way Chip and Gail became friends. In fact, they became best friends and were virtually inseparable throughout high school. Neither ever mentioned anything about getting romantically involved, nor did they actually "date" (though Chip claims he did tell Gail he knew

they'd get married some day). After they graduated, they continued to be just friends (just best friends, that is). Now that she was out of school, Gail's father told her she needed to get a job and move out. So, at the age of seventeen, Gail ended up sleeping on a mattress on the floor of a friend's mobile home. At this point, neither Chip nor Gail had any real faith in God. Actually, Chip was a Sunday school dropout, having been thrown out of class for being bad as a young boy. Gail remembered times when, as a child, she would cry out to God and ask for his help when things got rough at home.

One evening Chip and Gail were talking as they often did, but began to discuss their future. They both started to realize that their lives were being pushed together. At one point Chip looked at Gail and said, "I *told* you we were going to get married some day." The next day he took her to the store and bought her a ring. They were married four months later and the two teenagers moved into a mobile home of their own. It wasn't long before their first of two children was born, and it was shortly after that when I first met them. I was single at the time and had moved into the mobile home right next to theirs. We quickly became as close as family (which, in a trailer park, could be taken quite literally).

A few years later, when Jason was four years old, his grandmother (Gail's mom) passed away and the little boy was devastated. He began to ask his mom all kinds of questions about death, life after death, and God. Gail figured the best thing to do was be honest. "Honey, if you want to know about God, go ask Patty." I had just gotten out of the shower, was late for work, and was dripping wet when I heard someone knocking at the door. I threw on my bathrobe and peeked out the top window. There was no one there. I jumped when the knocking continued. I swung open the door and saw a sad little boy standing there looking up at me. "Hi, Jason! What can I do for you?" I asked. He looked into my eyes with as serious a face as I've ever seen on a four-year old and said, "I want to know about God."

So, a bit overwhelmed at the daunting task that faced me, I invited Jason in. Everything I'd ever learned about how to share

my faith suddenly vacated my mind. I started to fumble for words as I tried to explain to a four-year-old that God loves him ... "and if you ask him into your heart he will come in and take you to heaven to be with your grandmother when you die and ..." and right in the middle of my expository sermon, Jason turned, without saying another word, and walked out the door. I sighed, figuring I had totally confused him. I said a little prayer for him and continued to get ready for work. It wasn't until the next day that I discovered Jason had run home and gleefully announced to Gail, "Mommy, I've got Jesus in my heart! Do you have Jesus in your heart?" And not long after that Gail, too, had Jesus in her heart and was soon followed by Chip. As they look back today at the path that brought them together and to him, they now realize that the Lord had been working behind the scenes in their lives drawing them to each other and to himself all along.

Gail recently shared an example of this with me. Back when she was still living at home and in the middle of a particularly bad experience, Gail pulled out a pen and paper one night and wrote a letter to God. "God, I just want to be loved. I want someone to love me just for being me. I don't care what he looks like, or anything about his past. I just want someone who loves me, who I can raise a family together with. God, I want him to be my best friend...." She wrote several more pages pouring her heart out to God, describing all of the longings in her troubled heart. Then she sealed the envelope, put it away, and forgot about it. Almost 25 years later, Gail was going through some boxes and came across that letter. As she read it, she began to weep once again and pour her heart out to God. But this time it was tears of joy and words of thanksgiving as she realized that God had given her every request in that letter. If you ask Gail what the secret has been to their 25 wonderful years of marriage (which I did), she would tell you it is that they were friends first — best friends. And they are still best friends today. She would also tell you that they now have an even better best friend than each other. As Jesus put it, "My command is this: Love each other as I have loved you. Greater love has no one than this,

43

that he lay down his life for his friends ... I have called you friends" (John 15:12-15).

Chip and Gail still live in a mobile home in a trailer park. They could have bought a home by now, but helping put their two kids through college was much more important to them than owning a nice house. And even more important than that, they have each other. As the Love Chapter puts it, "Love is not proud." They aren't out to impress anyone. They are best friends and that is what matters most of all to them. Well, that, and their best friend, Jesus.

Love is best friends and friends forever in Christ.

Spilling Over With Grace

It is not rude. — 1 Corinthians 13:5a

Before I begin, I need you to understand that he never asked me *not* to do it. Honest! I'm sure that was due, in part, to all of my assurances that I have never tipped a boat in my life and could probably swim all the way to Canada if I needed to. But I think that, even more, it was because Bob knows how much I love to take pictures of the wonders I see while out in my kayak so I can come back and share them with him. If for no other reason than because it gives me joy, he simply wouldn't have refused me the opportunity to do so. That's just the way he is. At most, if I were to be completely honest, he might have mumbled something about it not being terribly safe to take an expensive camera out on a kayak. But he never asked me *not* to do it.

I had actually taken the camera out in the kayak with me several times before. This particular photo shoot was supposed to be no different than the rest. So just before what I was anticipating to be a gorgeous sunset on the horizon, I hauled my boat down to the dock, and while holding tightly onto the bowline I shoved it over the edge and into the water. Then I stood and watched in horror as the line unknotted itself and the kayak floated freely away down the river. After only a moment of hesitation, I did what any kayak-loving, river-blooded person would have done. I jumped off the dock into the water and swam after my fastly departing boat. I have to admit it was a breathtakingly well-executed rescue. I reached the boat in seconds and using my strongest lifesaving carry, brought it quickly and safely back to the dock. It was only as I triumphantly climbed out of the water dripping from head to foot that it hit me.

Bob's digital camera-that-cost-more-than-my-kayak was still in my now soaked pocket!

The horror I had felt over seeing the kayak float away couldn't begin to compare to the agony I was now experiencing. The reality of what I had done sank in even more quickly than the evening chill. At that moment I wanted nothing more than to climb in the kayak and float down the river never to be seen again. Instead, I put the boat away and headed back up to the camp. Bob had not seen what had just taken place and looked up from his book with surprise.

"Wow, that was a short trip," he said, though he immediately sensed something was wrong as I stomped past him in silence and headed into the cottage. Perhaps it was the pools of water I was trailing behind me, but I think it was the look of utter despair on my face. He followed me in after a few moments and found me sitting at the kitchen table, dripping wet with puddles forming around me, sobbing my eyes out.

At first, he was frightened that I had been hurt. I was crying so hard I couldn't get any words out but I finally managed to hand him the camera and blubber something about runaway boats, dramatic rescues, and ... soaked digital cameras. Now, the point in me retelling this humiliating story isn't to prove how stupid I am (at least, not the main point), but to share Bob's response. When I told him what I had done my dear husband's first thoughts were about my safety. "Are you okay? Did you hurt yourself?" I tried to explain that I was not hurt; I was just a wet idiot who had destroyed the expensive camera her beloved had entrusted to her care. Bob just brushed my words aside and calmly said, "You need to get out of those wet clothes before you catch a cold."

When I realized he had no intention of getting angry with me, I cried all the harder. "I'm so sorry, honey!" I blubbered. "I've ruined your camera." He told me not to worry, that it really was no big deal and again urged me to get myself dried off so I didn't get sick. Then he quietly took the camera from me and did his best to dry it off. He suggested we let it air out for a while and not try to use it for a day or so. But I think we both knew it was most likely

ruined and I felt that I had let him down. I asked him, once again, why he wasn't mad at me — why he didn't say, "I told you so" — why he was so forgiving. I felt completely unworthy of his gracious response and was having a hard time believing that he really wasn't angry. He assured me he wasn't. He said he loved me and that I was far more important to him than a camera. I realized that I simply needed to take him at his word and whispered a silent prayer of thanks for this precious gift of a husband God had blessed me with.

I also realized that God was using this incident to teach me a little lesson. It was a lesson on grace. Grace is, of course, amazing. I may have been able to tell you all of this before, but I suddenly understood it from within the depths of my heart. Grace is undeserved favor. It is getting something we do not deserve and not getting something we do deserve. I deserved a lecture on the importance of taking extra cautions with valuable equipment. I did not get that. I did not deserve someone overlooking my bad decision and looking only to my needs. That is grace. That is the same kind of grace God extends to every one of us who has messed up. We deserve condemnation. But all who ask receive forgiveness, unconditional love — grace.

God extends his love to the most unlikely people, according to the world's standards, and pours his grace upon them. He chooses those in the greatest need of forgiveness, to forgive. He takes the weakest and the most broken, and makes them strong and whole — the biggest failures, in the world's eyes, and transforms them into his greatest success stories. In so doing, he has made it perfectly clear that he does not love us because of anything we have done but solely because he is God and being God is, by nature, love. In fact, he loved us enough to die for us. And all we need to do, to experience that indescribable, incomparable love and grace is to take him at his word. When we take that step of faith and open our hearts to him, we find he is just waiting to share all of his love, forgiveness, and grace with us.

It is that same kind of grace we have received from him that he wants us to show to each other in our marriages. He urges us to

"Let your conversation be always full of grace, seasoned with salt, so that you may know how to answer everyone" (Colossians 4:6). Or, as the Love Chapter puts it, "Love is not rude." Now, one might say this is easier said than done (one might be right about that), but as we reflect on the *love* who faced his scoffers saying, "Father, forgive them, for they do not know what they are doing" (Luke 23:34) it all comes into focus. True love is all about grace. And that truly is amazing.

**Love tenderly looks past wrongs done,
through eyes of grace.**

The One That Didn't Get Away

Love ... is not self-seeking.   — 1 Corinthians 13:5b

Bob and I went fishing earlier this week. You'd think, having a camp on the Saint Lawrence Seaway, this would have been a routine occurrence for us but, in fact, this was the first time Bob and I have actually gone fishing ... at the same time ... together.

When Bob proudly pulled his first catch out of the river (it was a six-inch crappie), he was so excited that he asked me to take a picture of him posing with it. "This is the first fish I've caught in over thirty years!" he proudly announced. I looked nervously at the six-inch crappie hoping that I wasn't looking at the main course of a victory dinner. "Really, honey? That can't be true, can it?" I reminded him of how, not long after we had gotten married, he had gone out and bought us both fishing licenses, rods, tackle, and an impressive collection of goofy-looking lures. I'd never caught much with the goofy-looking lures but after he broke down and let me get a bucket of worms, I think I must have caught at least one representative of every species of fish in the Northeast. But as I was thinking back about it now, I realized that I had been the only one who ended up doing any fishing. Bob would come along, sit nearby, and contentedly alternate between reading a book and watching me while I fished.

After the photo shoot, Bob released the crappie who happily swam away apparently no worse for the wear. I breathed a silent sigh of relief, thankful that there would be no need to have to come up with a recipe for crappie squares. As we walked back to the house, the victorious fisherman and I, I asked Bob why, after spending all that money getting us fishing equipment back then, he had

never joined me and put a line in the water up until tonight. He thought about it a bit and replied, "I think it was because I just really enjoyed watching you fish. It was fun for me just seeing you look so happy and having such a good time." In fact, one of the main reasons he had gotten all that equipment in the first place was not as much out of his own burning desire to wave goofy-looking lures in the faces of disinterested fish, but because he knew that fishing was something I loved to do.

It wasn't until later that evening as I was having my devotions, that Bob's response hit me full force. I had always assumed that Bob had bought us all that fishing gear because he liked to fish. What probably came as a surprise, even to Bob, was that he had taken more pleasure simply in watching me doing something I enjoyed than in doing it himself. As I was warmly thinking about Bob's sweet response it occurred to me that the Lord, in much the same way, loves to give his beloved children good gifts and then delight in watching us enjoy them. I had been thinking about this earlier in the week while sitting by the lake. The scene before me was so lovely that I found myself pouring my heart out to God in wonder and awe over all the beauty he has created. As I continued to sit there by the water, I sensed that my spontaneous outburst of praise brought him great pleasure. It delighted him that I was enjoying his creation and that I wanted to share my joy with him. I think the psalmist must have had the same idea when he wrote, "The Lord was my support. He brought me out into a spacious place; he rescued me because he delighted in me" (Psalm 18:18-19). Imagine that! The creator of the universe delights in us! The scriptures tell us, "Sing, O Daughter of Zion; shout aloud, O Israel! Be glad and rejoice with all your heart, O Daughter of Jerusalem! ... The Lord your God is with you, he is mighty to save. He will take great delight in you, he will quiet you with his love, he will rejoice over you with singing" (Zephaniah 3:14, 17). While the thought may seem almost incomprehensible that the God of the universe delights in us and in pouring his blessings upon us, it does make sense. After all, who else of all of his creation did God

make in his own image, with the capacity to appreciate all the wonder and beauty of his creation? Who else did he create with the ability to recognize his fingerprints built into his creation and to respond to him in loving delight?

God created all of this marvelously beautiful, perfectly designed universe. Then, last of all, he created us. He then invited us to take part in his creation along with him. He placed Adam in the garden and told him "to work it and take care of it" (Genesis 2:15). He gave him the task of naming each of the animals and "whatever the man called each living creature, that was its name" (Genesis 2:19). And even after the Fall, God told him to "till the ground from whence he was taken" (Genesis 3:23). Jesus, himself, reaffirmed his great desire to share his creation with us telling his disciples, "Do not be afraid, little flock, for it is your Father's good pleasure to give you the kingdom" (Luke 12:32). So, indeed, from the beginning, God had us in mind when he created this wondrous world. Then, he rested. The creator of the universe sat back and took delight in watching us enjoy it!

Well, not really. God never actually sat back and just watched. He continues to be actively involved in his creation and he does it for us. He paints a beautiful sunset in the evening sky. He causes the flowers to bloom in the spring, and the birds to sing their glorious melodies. He starts each day with a glorious sunrise, and decorates the night sky with an infinite array of sparkling lights. In the same way, Bob found pleasure in seeing me use and enjoy the fishing equipment he got for me, it gives our Lord great joy when all of the marvelous works of his hands bring us delight. When we see all of his wonders, experience his countless blessings, and acknowledge they are all from him, our joyous response is true worship. And nothing delights him more than that!

Yes, as I sat there by the lake that night, gazing in wonder at the beauty before me and pouring my heart out in thanksgiving to the Lord, I sensed he was pleased — in fact, delighted that I was so enthralled with his creation. I think that is why, when Bob shared his fish story (or the reason behind the lack thereof), I was reminded of the kind of love God has for each of his children. True love finds

joy in seeing its lover happy. Or, even better, in making the other happy even at its own expense. And, oh, what an expense God went to on our behalf. Far beyond delighting us with the works of his hands, God stretched out those same hands, and allowed them to be nailed to a cross in the ultimate expression of selfless love. And when, in utter amazement, we respond to this act of indescribable love and worship him, nothing delights him more than that.

Love delights in putting the other's needs first.

The Perfect Storm

It is not easily angered. — 1 Corinthians 13:5c

I can honestly say, "I knew them when." In fact, I knew them even before they were a when. Lori and I went to the same church together for most of our lives. Greg joined our church singles group as a new believer. It was there where he first sensed God calling him into the ministry. It was also there at that singles group that he fell in love with Lori and they eventually got married. They are currently living happily ever after. But it wasn't always this way for them. They had to go through some rather stormy times to get to where they are today.

When Greg came to Christ, he underwent a radical transformation that took him, virtually overnight, from a life of alcohol, drugs, and country music ... well, I think he still likes country music. But other than that, God immediately delivered him from even the desire for alcohol or drugs (we're still praying about the country music). After they were married, they followed the Lord's leading and went to seminary after which Greg accepted a pastorate in New England. Things were going very well there, but when the opportunity arose for them to come back and pastor a church in the area where they both grew up, Greg gladly accepted the position. At first, things went great! The church doubled in four years under Greg's leadership and even needed to develop a building program to accommodate everyone. Then, just a week after the new building was completed, Greg walked into the elders meeting and was asked to resign. He was told that he didn't have what it takes to take the church to the next level of growth. When the congregation heard what happened, many were outraged and the church was

nearly ripped apart. Greg knew that if he did not resign immediately, the church would probably split. So, he quietly stepped down.

Greg had lost a job, but he soon realized he had lost much more than that. He felt as though he had lost it all — his ministry, their church family, their home, their friendships, his identity, his purpose, and his self-confidence. He felt betrayed and humiliated. Most of all, he felt like a failure. He felt he had failed his family, the church, and God, and it hurt more than anything he had ever experienced. Lori was also devastated by the situation so they went, together, to a Christian counselor to help them deal with their pain. Through counseling, Greg realized the rejection he felt from the church had brought out personal issues related to his childhood that he never realized he had. After hearing Greg's father had been an alcoholic, the counselor brought up the question of abuses in his childhood. Greg couldn't come up with any at first, but over the next few days, he began to remember all of the verbal assaults, threats, and fears that were an everyday part of his young life. And as he did, he saw the connection between his childhood and what had happened at the church. At one point, it was as if all forty years of suppressed emotions were released and he sobbed for the next hour.

Those were the most agonizing moments in Greg's life but they were also the most healing. Greg came to understand how he had developed unhealthy coping strategies. He had never learned how to express love or how to appropriately deal with anger. When he came to Christ, he was delivered from drugs and booze but never dealt with the buried emotions that had driven him to them. That is why God had allowed what Greg now refers to as the "perfect storm" in his life. Through losing his pastorate, Greg was forced to face all the emotions he had tucked away since childhood. But he wasn't forced to face them alone. Greg learned to trust the Lord as never before as the Lord brought him through the perfect storm and on to higher ground. There were some raging seas to be navigated but in time — in God's time — Jesus calmed the troubled waters and brought him true peace. Eventually, the healing was complete enough that Greg had a renewed desire to return to the pastorate.

So when the door of opportunity opened, Greg and Lori walked through it by faith and they are joyfully ministering together in a thriving church family today.

If you asked Greg why they had to go through what they did, he would most likely respond with a little of his "storm theology" that includes a lesson on God's recycling program. Greg and Lori learned that God allows pain to get our attention, to help us learn to depend on him, and then to give us a ministry to others. In other words, God recycles our pain. He uses our most difficult trials to prepare us to serve others. So, as Greg puts it, "the perfect storm is a perfecting storm that purifies our life and promotes healing that overflows to others."

Greg gives an example how God recycled pain in their marriage. Greg loves control and order. This became a major source of conflict between him and Lori early in their marriage. He would get angry and go into silent mode, and Lori would try to reconcile. They would resolve the issue and then move on until the cycle began again. Neither of them realized Lori was coming up against Greg's still-hidden childhood wounds. One day, a friend of Greg's began to describe what he referred to as "patterns of anger" he had discovered in his marriage. As he did, Greg realized that he, too, had a pattern of anger in his marriage that had hurt his wife for many years. He also realized he had never repented of it. He went home and immediately asked Lori's forgiveness. She told him she had already forgiven him but rejoiced that he had recognized it and shared it with her. The next morning, Greg began to weep as he thought about how his behavior had cost them so much joy in their marriage over the years. He came down and hugged Lori. He also made himself accountable to several pastor friends. If you were to meet this loving couple today, you would never suspect they ever struggled in this area. God's healing was complete. So complete, in fact, that Greg and Lori are now ministering to others. Their pain has been recycled. Yours can be, too. It starts by being willing to cry out to God in your pain, and to listen to his response with an open heart. The Holy Spirit will speak uniquely to your pain with his comfort, counsel, and conviction. As Greg puts it, "God can

speak at a depth you can't even imagine. And emotionally we see our lives getting to where God wants them to be. The joy of that is the intimacy in your marriage and the ability to cherish each other and nourish each other as God truly designed. So, listen with an open heart and the Holy Spirit will speak in your time of pain."

The Love Chapter states that love "is not easily angered." Greg learned through his perfect storm that we can hold a lot of hurts and anger inside us and not even realize we are doing it, until we release it on our spouses. But when we release it to God, he brings healing. The Lord allows the storms in our lives to bring healing to the wounds of the past and present and frees us to love each other, and others, with lives purified by the storm.

**Love allows the storms in life
to accomplish their perfect healing work.**

Sea No Evil

Love ... keeps no record of wrongs.
— 1 Corinthians 13:5d

It was a typical hot summer in Savannah, Georgia. Dave was stationed at the army base there and Karin, who would probably have preferred to live in a cooler environment like her hometown in Germany, was doing what most military wives do best — she was living with her husband in Savannah, Georgia. They didn't have a lot of money for extras back then (thinking about it, they still don't), so when the opportunity came along for Dave to have the use of a boat for the day, he jumped at it. Several of his buddies had gotten together to rent a small outboard boat on a trailer and had planned a "men's day out" fishing trip. When their plans fell through, and since the boat was already paid for, Dave got the idea of taking his beloved, overheated bride out for her own private ocean cruise. What could possibly be more romantic?

Whatever doubts or misgivings Karin may have had, she kept them to herself (for the most part). If Karin had learned nothing else in the few years they had been married, she had come to count on the fact that, whatever romantic idea Dave came up with, it was going to end up being an adventure.

Dave pulled up in front of the house with the boat in tow and told Karin to get in the car and not ask any questions. My guess is at that point she might have suspected what they were going to do. Nevertheless, she hopped in, and off they went. They were enjoying the ride together, or least they were, until Dave looked in the rear view mirror and saw the bow of the boat pointing almost straight upward. It had apparently come loose from the trailer hook. Just as

alarming was the look on the face of the man in the car right behind them. Thankfully, Dave realized what was happening before the boat had the opportunity to go airborne. He pulled off the road (as the car behind him flew past, its driver making some rather interesting hand symbols out the side window as it did) and got the boat tied securely in place. They continued on their way with no further incidents.

When they arrived at the dock, Dave had to back the trailer down the ramp as a crowd of onlookers watched. In less than twenty tries, he managed to steer the boat into the water. He parked the car and the two of them hopped in. As Dave turned the key, Karin calmly asked, "Dave, why is there so much water in the bottom of the boat?" Without looking back, Dave assured her that water in the bottom of boats is normal. She tried again, a little firmer this time. "Dave, the boat is filling up with water." At that point, Dave looked down and, sure enough, it was. Karin was bailing, with the only object she could find — a small styrofoam cup she had brought along in their picnic basket. Dave suddenly realized that now would be an excellent time to put the drain plug in.

Eventually, they were underway. It was a picture perfect day, the seas were calm, and after a while they came to a lovely little island where Dave lifted up the engine and let the boat run aground on the sandy beach. They sat there together for quite a while, losing track of time, munching on sandwiches, and enjoying each other's company. Suddenly, Dave noticed a large ship pass directly behind them in the rear view mirror. With no time to move, they braced themselves for the inevitable tsunami that was about to hit them, but after a few moments ... nothing. "Must not have made much of a wake after all," Dave assured Karin. But as they stood up and looked behind them, they realized that the reason they hadn't been hit by a wave is because the tide had gone out, leaving their boat on dry ground. For the next half hour or so, the two of them were outside the boat tugging and dragging it across the sand beach back to the water.

Finally, panting, sweating, and exhausted, they got their vessel afloat and underway. But not for long. They had only gone a short

distance when it stalled out. And it wouldn't start back up. "Now what?" he asked. Karin just rolled her eyes. He lifted up the engine and found the propeller completely wound up in the stern line (the rope that should have been inside the boat but somehow ended up outside the boat). As he wrestled with the lines Karin offered, "Dave, why don't we go back now? I think I've had enough fun for one day." Dave wouldn't hear of it. "No, we are here to have a good time, and we are going to stay out here in this boat until we do." Karin knew that when Dave had that look of determination in his eyes, there was simply no turning back. Once the line was untangled, Dave turned the key and the engine started right up. He cranked it up full throttle and the two lovebirds spent the rest of the afternoon cruising the high seas in wedded bliss.

When they returned, just before sunset, Dave had been hoping the crowds would have died down so he could ramp in a bit more inconspicuously. No such luck. Word must have gotten out after his dramatic entry earlier in the day because (or so he claims), there were multitudes of people standing there with no other purpose than to gawk as he attempted to navigate a smooth landing onto the trailer. He backed the car down, got into the boat, and discovered the wind was making for a rather strong current. With the pressure on, the crowds staring, and his beloved looking on somewhat skeptically, he made his approach. He felt the current dragging the boat back out to sea, so he gunned it. It was, perhaps, one of the first things that actually went smoothly. The boat slipped onto the trailer and the crowds roared. (Well, actually, no one was really paying all that close attention — I think Dave was a bit disappointed.)

As they drove home, laughing over all the mishaps they had survived, they both agreed it was one of the best days they'd had in a long time. The point to Dave and Karin's nautical adventure is that they were able to turn a day of disasters into a day of fond memories. Peter wrote, "Above all, love each other deeply, because love covers over a multitude of sins" (1 Peter 4:8). Granted, forgetting to put the plug in the bottom of the boat isn't quite on the level of the unforgivable sin, but the point is well taken. The scriptures

also tell us, "Those with good sense are slow to anger, and it is their glory to overlook an offense" (Proverbs 19:11 NRSV). There were plenty of opportunities for Dave and Karin to have gotten frustrated, angry, and even bail out of their day (and their boat) altogether. But they had learned, and continue 25 years later, to look past the blunders and mistakes each of them may make and look, instead, for the blessings. The blessing of that day was precious time spent together. And of course, just as Karin expected, an adventure.

Love looks past the mess ups to find the blessings.

United We Stand

Love does not delight in evil. — 1 Corinthians 13:6a

They had just gotten back from a year in the mission field. The whole family, Rob, Barb, and their two girls, had lived together in a tiny hut in the middle of South America. They loved seeing what God was doing there among the natives, but living in a foreign culture also knit them together as a family in a very special way. That closeness was what made the trials of the year ahead all the more difficult. Having sold their home, they had no place to stay when they arrived in the states. With the new school year fast approaching, Barb felt her nesting instincts reaching a level of desperation. That is why, when they found the duplex located in a good school district, she pushed Rob to take it even against his better judgment. Looking back on it today, Barb realizes it was partly due to her unwillingness to defer to her husband that they ended up in a situation that nearly tore their family apart.

The family in the other half of the duplex had a son the same age as their oldest daughter, Katie. Unknown to Rob and Barb at the time, they were a very troubled family, both of the parents having been abused as children. Though they loved their son, their own wounds had deep effects on Sam. None of this was evident at first. Katie and Sam became fast friends. Once school started, they were inseparable. At school and after school, they were always together. It wasn't long before they started dating. The first sign of trouble appeared in Sam's responses to Rob (and subsequently all male authority figures). He was rude and defiant. Over time, Rob and Barb started to express concern to Katie, which only seemed to push them closer together. Their sweet daughter who had shared

a single hut with them less than a year earlier gradually became distant, hardened, and rebellious. As the young couple continued to spend vast amounts of time together Rob and Barb tried to establish some boundaries. The question was, was it too late?

Sam's reaction to the new limitations soon translated into secret meetings, deceitfulness, and manipulation. Katie often tried to pit Barb against Rob to get her way. Her personality had changed so drastically that Barb and Rob sought professional counseling for her. After a few sessions with Katie, the counselor (a Christian) asked Rob and Barb if they had considered the possibility of this being spiritual oppression. Barb had told her how at times she would be talking to her daughter who she loved and then at other times felt she didn't even know her. The counselor suggested that Rob and Barb begin to pray for discernment.[1] Through prayer, they came to realize that their beloved daughter was, indeed, being oppressed by spirits of anger, fear, and rebellion. Getting her back would require spiritual warfare. If the battle was to be won, it must be fought, first and foremost, with prayer.[2]

Rob now realized they needed to move out of the duplex for the safety of their family. This time, he got no objections from Barb. She had known all along that God protects families when they are under the husband's covering. She also knew that they needed to be completely united as they fought this battle. Getting through this would require tough love — tougher than she could give on her own. She needed Rob's strength. "I knew we needed to strictly hold to the boundaries we had set but they were so difficult for us to keep. As she continued to break the rules and her freedoms were taken away I told Rob, 'Honey, you need to help me. I need to do the right thing but this hurts so much.'" Barb knew that the strength and love of both parents would be critical if they were to get through this. They needed to be united as a couple. Divided they would fall.

After they moved, they decided it would be best to not allow Katie to see Sam at all. It wasn't long before Katie's despondency and her relentlessly seething anger weakened their resolve. They agreed to make a contract with her to allow her and Sam to

see each other, but only in their presence and at their house. It was a complete disaster. Sam ended screaming at Rob that "as soon as she turns eighteen she is coming with me and you will never see her again." Barb watched in horror as Katie looked on in full agreement.

When they told the counselor, she was firm: "You need to be able to fight this to the death." She explained that they needed to accept the possibility of their worst-case scenario and then do the right thing anyway. Barb admitted that her greatest fear was that Katie would run off with Sam, get pregnant, and she would never see her again. Rob was most afraid that she would become so depressed she would commit suicide. Together, they faced their greatest fears and then committed them, and Katie, to God. Then, they committed themselves to do the right thing. Hand-in-hand, with tears streaming down their faces, they prayed, "God, Katie is yours. If we try to hang on to her, we will lose this battle. She is not ours, but yours." After they prayed, Rob and Barb felt a great peace. A huge burden had been lifted from their battle-weary shoulders. Nevertheless, the battle continued.

Despite all the boundaries, Katie attempted to find ways to secretly meet with Sam. Sensing this, Rob followed her one night and found her bike parked next to Sam's car. Too angry to face them by himself, Rob went back and got Barb and returned just in time to see them parting ways. Sam caught Rob's eye and defiantly drove away. Rob ordered Katie to get into the car. She was literally stiff with rage. They started to drive home in silence. Barb quietly cried out to the Lord for his help. Suddenly, Rob pulled the car over to the side of the road, looked over at Katie and said, "In Jesus' name I want to talk to my daughter, not the spirit that is harassing my daughter." Katie's body immediately relaxed, and she began to sob hysterically. Her whole demeanor changed. She begged her parents to forgive her. The three of them fell into each other's arms and wept.

This was not the end of Rob and Barb's fight for their daughter, but it was the turning point in the battle. There would be several additional incidents but from that point on the hold Sam had

on Katie began to be released. A few years later, in her freshman year of college Katie, recommitted her life to Christ and never looked back. Today, she is engaged to a wonderful Christian man. Rob and Barb have their beloved daughter back.

Barb knows without a doubt that had she and Rob not been united — in mind, in spirit, and in Christ — they would have lost the battle for their daughter. Because they were willing, as a team, to surrender her back to God and then fight for her on their knees in prayer, God honored their faith and gave them the victory. If you ask Barb (I did), she would say it was well worth the battle. God not only restored their relationship with their daughter but he deepened their love for each other. Their hearts have been united together as one — Rob, Barb, and him.[3]

**Love fights for its family as a united team
(husband, wife, and Christ), and wins.**

1. Two books that their counselor recommended that they found very helpful were Mark I. Bubeck's *Raising Lambs Among Wolves: How To Protect Your Children From Evil* (Chicago: Moody Publisher, 1997) and Henry Cloud and Dr. John Townsend's *Boundaries With Kids* (Grand Rapids, Michigan: Zondervan, 2001).

2. See 2 Corinthians 10:3-4 and Ephesians 6:11-18.

3. A cord of three strands is not quickly broken (Ecclesiastes 4:12).

A Love Affair

Love ... rejoices with the truth.

— 1 Corinthians 13:6b

After having been out of touch for over twenty years, I recently reconnected with a friend from college. It was wonderful catching up on each other and the different paths our lives had taken since then. However, some of what my friend had been through since we last talked came as quite a shock to me. She would be the first to say that God used the course of events to make her who she is and I would have to say that she is a woman of great faith.

Back in college, Sharry* had always had a secret crush on Derrick*. But then, so did many of the other girls on campus. When she told me she had ended up marrying him my initial response was something to the effect of "Wow!" She laughed and explained how, after college, he had gone on to get his master's degree in the same town where she was living. What had started out as a convenient friendship ended up with a marriage proposal. That same year they moved across the country to where Derrick got his first job — a high paying position in a large national 401(k) corporation. They found a wonderful church and both Sharry and Derrick became actively involved in the ministry there. Derrick remained at that job for the next four years over which time they bought their own home and had two beautiful children. As far as Sharry was concerned, life was everything she had ever dreamed it could be.

Derrick was eventually offered a management position in another state. Though they were sad to leave the area and the church they loved so much, after praying about it together, they felt the

Lord leading them to make the move. It was shortly after they had settled in to their new home that Sharry's idyllic world came crashing down around her. One night after the children went to bed, Derrick told her he needed to tell her something that was going to be very difficult for him to share. As he had been praying that morning, the Spirit persuaded him that he needed to confess the secret sin he had been hiding from Sharry for the past several years. Actually, the Spirit had been compelling him to confess ever since it happened. Tears were now streaming down Derrick's face as he admitted that shortly after they were married he had an affair with another woman. He began to sob and to beg for Sharry's forgiveness. Sharry had never felt so lost and alone before in her life. All kinds of thoughts passed through her mind: "Who was it? How could you do this to me? What's wrong with me?" She felt rage, guilt, and a host of other emotions as she watched her husband openly weeping before her. She knew all the verses about forgiveness but at the moment she was too crushed — too devastated — to even consider them. She finally looked at Derrick and quietly responded, "I need time to think about all of this. I ... I just need to be alone right now." And with that, Sharry went upstairs, closed the bedroom door, fell on the bed, and wept uncontrollably.

Now, I doubt that a story about unfaithfulness in marriage is new to anyone. There are two reasons that Sharry and Derrick's situation is unique, and why their story is worth telling.

First, it is (far too) common for people to be caught in the act of adultery. It is rare that the guilty party freely confesses, not because they were discovered, but out of conviction and a desire to be right with God. Derrick was so sensitive to the Spirit's voice that he could no longer keep silent about what he had done. He knew he risked deeply hurting Sharry, and possibly even losing her by telling her what he had done. But it was the risk he knew he must take if he were to have a pure heart before her and God. The psalmist describes perfectly what Derrick was going through:

> *When I kept silent, my bones wasted away through my*
> *groaning all day long. For day and night your hand*

was heavy upon me; my strength was sapped as in the heat of summer. Selah. Then I acknowledged my sin to you and did not cover up my iniquity. I said, "I will confess my transgressions to the Lord" — and you forgave the guilt of my sin. — Psalm 32:2-5

Second, and the reason their story belongs in a book on love and marriage, is because the affair did not end in divorce. It ended in forgiveness, healing, and restoration. Sharry ultimately chose to forgive Derrick. She took the scriptures seriously that we are to forgive all who sin against us. How much more, then, the one she loved the most. She knew — they both knew — that it would not be easy getting over such a devastating betrayal of trust. But they also knew that God would give them the grace they needed to keep their marriage together. Derrick and Sharry recommitted themselves to each other, and to their loving Savior, following his admonition to, "love each other deeply, because love covers over a multitude of sins" (1 Peter 4:8). In time, it did. They were able to move past the wounds to have a strong and thriving marriage and family.

You almost never hear a story of marital unfaithfulness ending like Sharry and Derrick's. Either one partner will leave the marriage for the new lover, or the offended partner will refuse to take the guilty one back. That's the norm. But the Bible offers us a better way. In fact, God demonstrated the better way, himself. The book of Hosea tells the dramatic story of a man who God commanded to knowingly marry a prostitute. In obedience to God, Hosea married Gomer. They even had several children together. Then she went back to her old ways and left him for another lover. Hosea had every reason to divorce her. He had one reason not to — he loved her. So he went after her, right to the home of the lover, and paid a price to gain her back. It is a shockingly beautiful love story with a happy ending and the point God was making through it is that it is a picture of the kind of love he has for us. Even after his people were unfaithful to him, he cried, "How can I give you up? ... My heart recoils within me; my compassion grows warm and tender" (Hosea 11:8 NRSV). Even though each of us have

been unfaithful to him, God still loves us, too. In fact, he's wild about us — so much that he was willing to pay the ultimate price — his very life — to get us back.

The book of Hosea ends with a promise. After describing Hosea's passionate pursuit of his adulterous wife, God assures us that even if we have been unfaithful to him, if we would only return to him, "I will heal their waywardness and love them freely, for my anger has turned away from them" (Hosea 14:4). Sharry and Derrick learned firsthand how devastating unfaithfulness is in marriage. They also learned what it means to confess to one another and experience forgiveness and the healing power of God's love. They went through some extremely difficult times to get there, but they'd be the first to tell you it was worth it.

Love keeps no secrets but confesses to one another.

* These are not their real names. I have given them new names.

Batman To The Rescue

Love ... always protects.   — 1 Corinthians 13:7a

Everyone loves a good "damsel in distress" story but it is all the more intriguing when the tale takes place in the setting of a castle. Such is the love story of Harvey and Flo. Now, before I share this romantic and absolutely true story with you, let me give you a bit of background to properly set the stage. Harvey and Flo have just recently celebrated their fiftieth wedding anniversary. They have who-knows-how-many children, grandchildren, and great-grandchildren. It was shortly after the last of the children left the nest that they took up camping — tenting, to be specific. On one of their trips to their favorite campground in the Thousand Islands, they heard about Sunday services being held at Jorstadt Castle, a real castle located on one of the islands. Services were open to anyone who could get there by boat. The owners, Dr. H. G. Martin and his wife, Eloise, both Moody Bible College graduates, were the owners of the castle and were using it for evangelistic church services. The Martins loved to involve the worshipers in the services. That's how I ended up being the singer and piano player there for almost twenty years. That is also how Harvey eventually became the pastor. When the elderly Martins' health began to fail, making it impossible for them to run the services any longer, they asked Harvey if he would be willing to take them over. The offer included having him and Flo live on the island and maintain the castle throughout the week. So, they literally went from tents to turrets overnight. For the next fifteen years Harvey and Flo spent their summers running the Sunday services (along with the piano player who came in the package deal) and living in a castle.

The story sounds idyllic so far, but Harvey and Flo soon learned there is one drawback to living in a castle. That would be the bats. The Martins had, perhaps not accidentally, forgotten to mention the bats when they made their generous offer. But anyone who has ever lived in a castle could tell you that castles come with bats. Jorstadt proved to be no exception.

It was a lovely warm evening. They had had an exhausting day (anyone who has ever lived in a castle could also tell you they take a lot of work to maintain) and wanted nothing more than a good night's sleep. They turned out the lights and were soon sound asleep — but not for long. Harvey heard it first, a flapping sound swooping around the room. Deciding there was no need to upset his lovely bride of fifty plus years (and having learned after fifty plus years what *not* to wake her up over), he just pulled the sheets up to his chin and tried to remain inconspicuous (also known, in bat terminology, as lying under the radar). It is possible that he could have made it through until sunrise had the bat not swooped so low that it brushed against his face. That was going too far. Harvey flipped on the light and leapt out of bed! He grabbed the official bat-removal device he kept nearby, which looked quite similar to one of the castle rugby sticks (this wasn't their first encounter, by the way), and spent the next twenty minutes or so running around the room playing midnight rugby with the bat. Flo, who was wide awake at that point, played "ref." "He's over there. Get him. No, over there. A little higher. You missed. Don't hurt him." (Anyone happily married gets the idea.) Finally, in the last inning, score tied, Harvey did an end run, caught the bat in the rugby stick, and made the goal, releasing the bat out the window. The crowds, or at least Flo, roared!

Completely worn out from his great victory, the proud warrior crawled back into bed proud to have come to the rescue of his fair maiden once again. The two love birds were soon back to sleep. Flo claims it was no less than fifteen minutes later that she was awakened by the sensation of something clinging to the back of her head. She shouted at the top of her lungs: "It's on me! The bat is on my head! He is biting me!" She flew to an upright position and as Harvey flipped on the light he saw the evil creature fall from

her head and dive under the bed. The mighty warrior again boldly jumped into action — this time coming to the aid of his beloved bride who sat in bed screaming hysterically — "Get him! He's under the bed!" Harvey reached for his weapon and fearlessly (well, so he claims), bent down by the bed, ready to do battle face to face with the creature that had attacked his woman! Flo watched with horror as he bent low enough to see under the dark bed, rugby stick poised and ready, knowing the evil that lurked therein.

She watched as his face turned from intense determination to a quivering smile. He dramatically rammed the stick under the bed and exclaimed, "Fear not! I have captured it! You are safe!" Then, he pulled out the stick and proudly showed off his prize — a pair of false teeth! Flo had somehow gone to sleep with her dentures under her pillow and they had gotten caught in her hair. "I'm only glad I didn't have to hurt them. They came out without a fight," Harvey boasted before the two of them burst into laughter. The point of this little tale, of course, is that the king of the castle went to "bat" for his damsel in distress in her time of need. Though, he gets just a little less credit for his dramatic rescue since the first thing he did the next morning was to call all the grandkids to share the story.

Most of us will probably never have to defend our spouses from the attack of swooping bats or even carnivorous dentures. But all of us have been called to protect our spouses from anything, or anyone, threatening our marriages. Paul wrote,

> *Husbands, love your wives, just as Christ loved the church and gave himself up for her to make her holy, cleansing her by the washing with water through the word, and to present her to himself as a radiant church, without stain or wrinkle or any other blemish, but holy and blameless. In this same way, husbands ought to love their wives as their own bodies. He who loves his wife loves himself. After all, no one ever hated his own body, but he feeds and cares for it, just as Christ does the church.* — Ephesians 5:25-29

Think of it this way — Christ has invited us, as married couples, to play the leading roles in a drama far more exciting than even that of a castle rescue. He has called us to model the love that he, himself, has demonstrated for his church. He performed the ultimate in dramatic rescues, delivering his beloved bride from certain death through laying down his own life for her. Then, he gave us the incomprehensible privilege of reenacting that same kind of sacrificial love to each other in our marriages. Each time we come to each other's aid or choose to put our spouse's safety or well being over our own, we are imitating the love of Christ for all the world to see. We are also strengthening the marital bond between us, while building a castle wall that will help protect our marriage from anything that tries to threaten it. Except, maybe, for bats.

Love protects each other against all attacks.

Trusting To The Uttermost

Love ... always trusts.   — 1 Corinthians 13:7b

When I first met Dan and Debbie, Dan was a choir director at a large church in Mississippi. Their family was almost as large as the church — Dan and Debbie had nine children. Dan had been in his position at the church for almost seven years. While he enjoyed his music ministry, even when we first met the seeds of change were starting to take root deep within his spirit. You see, as musically gifted as Dan was, music was not his first love. No, you might say (I know I have) that Dan was born to preach. He had pastored several different churches over the years but when he left his last pastorate, far from home and with nine children to provide for, he and Debbie had decided to take some time off preaching, and move closer to where both of their families lived. That is where he found the position as music minister. It was a good paying job where he was serving the Lord and using the musical talent he had been given. It was a perfect situation. Except for one small thing — Dan was born to preach. So, when he started to get the itch once again, he knew it was God calling him back into the ministry — the ministry that his heart had never truly left.

After taking about it with Debbie (who wasn't the least bit surprised) and spending some time in prayer, he spiffed up his résumé and decided to see what door the Lord might choose to open for him to do what he loved best — telling people about Jesus Christ. Of course the most logical place to start in any job hunt is "Jerusalem" (also known as your own backyard).[1] So he sent a letter out to several ... well, actually a whole bunch of churches in the area to see if any of them were looking for a pastor. They weren't.

Not any of them. So, moving to "Judea" he broadened his search to a wider area. Still nothing. At this point he had one of two options: give up the dream and stick with choir directing (never a serious option — in fact, at this point he had resigned) or head for the uttermost parts of the earth. Though I might have considered it an insult to think of it that way at the time, it turned out that the uttermost parts ended up being New York state.

Living in New York and wanting to do anything I could to help Dan and Debbie (and their nine children), I did a little searching in my own Jerusalem and found a few interesting possibilities. One that I almost overlooked was a listing by a church so tiny I had doubts as to whether the whole family would even fit in the building. But there was something about the ad that was intriguing:

> *PASTORAL SEARCH: small church in New York seeks Pastoral Leader-Teacher to fill vacancy. Located in the foothills of the Adirondack Mountains, our attendance varies from 60-70 in summer to 40-50 in winter. If you preach-teach from the Bible and enjoy a loving congregation we would love to hear from you.*

What would a family of eleven, from a big city down south want with a country church in northern New York? But Dan decided to contact them and the little church from New York decided to respond. And the next thing they knew, Dan and Debbie and the six youngest children had packed up their car and were headed to New York (the theme song from *Green Acres* comes to mind).

Debbie and I talked at various stages of the adventure that dragged her away from the place she had grown up but I never sensed fear or disappointment. She seemed genuinely at peace following Dan wherever he went, with children in tow. But some time after the move I decided to ask Debbie again what it had been like to pull up roots, leave her whole family and even three of her precious children behind, and move to a place so small it isn't on the map. What was really going on in her heart? Was she really at peace throughout the whole ordeal? When I asked her if the move

had been difficult for her she answered with complete honesty. "No, it really wasn't. You see, God told me very clearly, 'Debbie, you need to trust me to lead Dan.' "

Debbie told me one other way God confirmed this message to her. As it was nearing time for them to leave for New York, her grandfather went into the hospital. The night before they left, Debbie went to visit him one last time. He took her hand, looked her in the eyes and said, "Debbie, I love you. Now, you gotta go where God wants you to go, and you gotta do what God wants you to do." Ten days after they arrived in New York, he went home to be with the Lord. Debbie realized that God, in his great love, had given them those special last moments together to say their good-byes. She also knew that God used her grandfather to confirm what God had already told her: "Trust me to lead Dan."

Debbie truly had a complete peace about going wherever Dan's ministry took him because she had the full assurance that God would faithfully lead Dan to where he wanted him to be. And when Debbie surrendered her desires to God by faithfully following her husband, she had complete confidence that he would provide. She told me that in situations like this (this wasn't the first move across the fruited plain, by the way), God has reminded her of Abraham and Sarah. When God told Abraham to pack his bags and go move into the desert, Sarah didn't even have the luxury of a parsonage to raise her children in. In fact, she didn't even have a child until she was ninety years old. Debbie told me, "You know, we don't hear much about Sarah's feelings but we do know God was faithful and never let her down."

I asked if she had any moments of doubt after arriving at Uttermost, New York. She told me that after having only been in their new home a week, still living out of boxes, far from her parents, and not knowing anyone in the congregation yet, she went to bed one night and silently whispered, "This just doesn't feel like home, Lord." She immediately sensed his answer: "Not yet, Debbie, but it will." She thanked him and drifted contentedly off to sleep.

It's been about two years since the move. Dan and Debbie and the children recently returned from their first visit to their families

in Tennessee. I asked Debbie how it felt to go back home after being away for so long. I was amazed at her response. "Patty, it was great to see our families, our parents, and our other children, but I can't tell you how good it was to finally get back home" (she was talking about New York, by the way). God had told Debbie: "Trust me to lead Dan." Debbie trusted, and discovered that one can even feel at home in the uttermost parts of New York.

Love trusts God to lead through her partner.

1. "But ye shall receive power, after that the Holy Ghost is come upon you: and ye shall be witnesses unto me both in Jerusalem, and in all Judea, and in Samaria, and unto the uttermost part of the earth" (Acts 1:8 KJV).

A *Good* Laugh

Love ... always hopes.   — 1 Corinthians 13:7c

Life was good! Abram and Sarai had just about everything a young couple could want in life. They lived near both of their extended families, they owned property, had extensive wealth, servants, and earthly possessions. Granted, they didn't have any children yet, but other than that they had it made. Or so they thought, until the day God decided to have a little talk with Abram. With no forewarning, the Lord told Abram to pack his bags and go. And at the time, he didn't even specify where. He told him, "Leave your country, your people and your father's household and go to the land I will show you" (Genesis 12:1). He did, however, give Abram a hint as to his ultimate purpose. In fact, he made him a promise saying, "I will make you into a great nation and I will bless you; I will make your name great, and you will be a blessing" (Genesis 12:2). As for Sarai, as Debbie said in the last chapter, we simply aren't told what she was thinking or feeling. All we know is that when Abram went, Sarai went with him and thus the adventure began. By the way, Abram was 75 and Sarai was 65 as they headed off to only-God-knows-where.

When they reached their destination, the land to which the Lord had directed them, there was no five-star hotel with a reservation in their name. In fact, the land of Canaan was, as one might have guessed, already occupied by the Canaanites. All Abram and Sarai had was a promise and a tent. They set up camp and just waited to see what would happen next. What happened next was a famine. So, they packed their bags once again and headed to Egypt to ride out the famine. As they approached Egypt, Abram, being the great

man of faith that he was, suggested to Sarai that she should tell everyone she was his sister and not his wife. He was worried that someone might decide they wanted her for themselves (she was a stunningly beautiful woman even at 65) and try to kill him. Again, we don't know what Sarai thought of that plan. But we are told she honored Abram's request even to the point where she ended up in the palace of Pharaoh who obviously had interests beyond reading her travel diary. However, God was faithful to Sarai and to Abram, and got them out of that mess and headed safely back to their Canaanite campground.

The happy campers remained there in Canaan for almost 25 years. Abram was now 99 years old and Sarai was pushing ninety. The Lord appeared to him and reminded him of his original promise: "You will be the father of many nations. No longer will you be called Abram; your name will be Abraham, for I have made you a father of many nations. I will make you very fruitful; I will make nations of you, and kings will come from you. I will establish my covenant as an everlasting covenant between me and you and your descendants after you for the generations to come" (Genesis 17:4-7). He continued on, "As for Sarai your wife, you are no longer to call her Sarai; her name will be Sarah. I will bless her and will surely give you a son by her. I will bless her so that she will be the mother of nations; kings of peoples will come from her" (Genesis 17:15-16). At this point Abraham, still being the godly man of faith that he was, had a good laugh. In fact, we are told he "fell face down; he laughed and said to himself, 'Will a son be born to a man a hundred years old? Will Sarah bear a child at the age of ninety?' " (Genesis 17:17). Despite Abraham's apparent amusement, God confirmed that this is exactly what he was going to do saying, "Yes, but your wife Sarah will bear you a son, and you will call him Isaac. I will establish my covenant with him as an everlasting covenant for his descendants after him" (Genesis 17:19).

If either of them still had any doubts, God personally stopped by the tent of Abraham and Sarah to say it one more time. Once again he told Abraham, "I will surely return to you about this time next year, and Sarah your wife will have a son" (Genesis 18:10).

Now it was Sarah's turn to laugh. We read, "Now Sarah was listening at the entrance to the tent, which was behind him ... Sarah laughed to herself as she thought, 'After I am worn out and my master is old, will I now have this pleasure?' " (Genesis 18:11-12).

So, Abraham and Sarah both had a good laugh over the thought of a 100-year-old man, and a ninety-year-old woman having a baby. Wouldn't you? But in his grace, God was not deterred by their laughter. The scriptures tell us, "Now the Lord was gracious to Sarah as he had said, and the Lord did for Sarah what he had promised. Sarah became pregnant and bore a son to Abraham in his old age, at the very time God had promised him" (Genesis 21:1-2). I can't help but to think that at this point, it was God who was now laughing — with delight.

After reading the adventures of Abraham and Sarah, one could reach the conclusion that God uses painfully real, blemished, and imperfect people to accomplish his greatest plans. They doubted, they lied, and they even laughed at God when he made his promises to them. Though, to be honest, if we put ourselves in their place would we have responded any differently? Probably not. Yet, the scriptures hold this couple up as an example of faith. In the "Faith Chapter" of the Bible, sometimes referred to as the "Faith Hall of Fame," we read, "By faith Abraham, even though he was past age — and Sarah herself was barren — was enabled to become a father because he considered him faithful who had made the promise. And so from this one man, and he as good as dead, came descendants as numerous as the stars in the sky and as countless as the sand on the seashore" (Hebrews 11:11-12).

Even in the most impossible of situations, laughter and all, Abraham and Sarah never lost hope in God. And God never disappoints those who hope in him. We are told, "Against all hope, Abraham in hope believed and so became the father of many nations, just as it had been said to him, 'So shall your offspring be.' Without weakening in his faith, he faced the fact that his body was as good as dead — since he was about a hundred years old — and that Sarah's womb was also dead. Yet he did not waver through

unbelief regarding the promise of God, but was strengthened in his faith and gave glory to God" (Romans 4:18-20).

Speaking of laughing, we are told that, just as God had told him to a year earlier, Abraham named his son Isaac which means, "he laughs." And how appropriate that was! When Sarah looked down at that precious bundle in her ninety-year-old lap, she laughed once again saying, "God has brought me laughter, and everyone who hears about this will laugh with me" (Genesis 21:6). Abraham and Sarah, despite their human weaknesses and failings, knew that God is faithful and that he keeps his promises. They hoped against all hope, in him, and you might say they got the last laugh.

**Love never loses hope even
when a situation looks impossible.**

Potholes And Perseverance

Love ... always perseveres.   — 1 Corinthians 13:7d

My old ... (well, not *that* old) ... college roommate and I have kept in touch on and off over the past never-mind-how-many years since graduation. I recently dropped her an email to check in, and it turned out that it happened to be the very day of her twenty-sixth wedding anniversary. Wow! Maybe we really are old roommates. When Pam and I graduated neither of us had even met our respective husbands at that time. She met her husband shortly after graduation and has been happily married ever since. Or, at least I assumed she was happily married. Knowing Pam, I didn't see how she could be anything but happy in her marriage. But since it was her anniversary and all, I decided I would ask. Having been her roommate I should have figured that with Pam there's no such thing as a yes/no answer. She wrote the following story.

My husband and I have been married 26 years. I'm an oldest child, he's a youngest. When we were first married, we had quite a few stormy encounters. I tried to assert my type A, oldest child personality over his type B, manipulating youngest child personality. We loved each other, but sparks did fly! As the years have gone by, we've both mellowed quite a bit, or gotten used to each other's habits, and the storms have subsided. I don't remember the last time we had an argument, and disagreements are minor.

I would say that we realized how much we thought alike a few years ago (not more than six or seven) when we gave each other

our anniversary cards. As usual, we both found our cards waiting on the kitchen counter the morning of August 29, and proceeded to open them. As we pulled them out of the envelopes, we both looked at each other with silly grins. You see, we had purchased the same card for each other! I don't remember what the card said — something silly, I'm sure — but we suddenly realized that Christ had truly made us one! I never cease to be amazed at how much our likes and dislikes have grown together. We are still individual in the things we do, but have learned to enjoy each other's company and doing some things together.

Too many couples decide to throw in the towel before they ever reach that point of likeness. When we married, we took the word "divorce" out of our vocabulary and never considered it an option, no matter how angry we got. I will admit that there were nights when we went to bed angry, but God was always the center of our lives, and with him as our magnet, we were always drawn back together. I would pray that more couples would take the time to see the humor in the situations that arise in their lives, and turn more often to God to steady their lives, instead of blaming each other or others for the bumps in the road. Just as we travel in our cars and often hit potholes or bumps, so it is with our married lives. Potholes and bumps arise, but with Christ as the repairman, we can't go wrong!

As I read Pam's story, I found myself smiling. I wouldn't have expected her thoughts on marriage to be any other way. You see, I once had the opportunity to personally experience Pam's commitment to potholes and bumps for myself. Though we were friends throughout our four years in college, we were not roommates for the first three years. I was rooming with two other girls. That is, until I got sick. Somewhere around the end of my first year in college I developed anorexia nervosa and I basically stopped eating. At that time, there was little known about this disease and

everyone (including me) pretty much hoped I would eventually just snap out of it. But by the end of my third year, my weight had dropped dangerously low and I was doing even worse emotionally. I can only imagine how difficult it must have been for my two roommates who had to helplessly watch me go steadily downhill. It is no wonder that at the end of the year the two of them sadly told me they could no longer deal with being my roommates. I would have to find someone else to live with for my final year of college. I was devastated. I knew it was not their fault but I felt totally abandoned with nowhere to turn. I went over to the music building with tears streaming down my cheeks, crying out to God to show me what to do. The first person I ran into as I entered the building was Pam. She saw how upset I was and asked me what was wrong and I blurted out, "No one wants to be my roommate next year." Without even pausing to think, she looked into my eyes and said, "I want to be your roommate. Will you room with me next year?"

I hardly knew what to say. Pam knew how sick I was. She had to know how difficult it might be. It wasn't until several years after graduating college that I asked her about that remarkable day and what she was thinking at the time. I wish I could remember the exact words she said (but I know that being Pam, there were no doubt a lot of them). But the gist of what she said was that I was her friend, she saw I had a need, and that friends don't abandon each other even when the going gets rough. She also saw something in me that, at the time, I didn't even see in myself. She sensed God had a special purpose for me (I bet she never imagined it might be to share this story for the world to read).

Pam and I roomed together for our last year of college, and it *was* a difficult year for the both of us. My illness created more potholes and bumps than I am guessing she had bargained for. But she later told me she never regretted the decision of rooming together and never once thought of backing out. Friends don't give up on each other even when the going gets rough. That is why I smiled when I read her 26-year tribute to her marriage. Of course, throwing in the towel would not be an option for Pam and her

husband, nor was the "d" word a part of their vocabulary. God has honored their commitment with 26 years and counting of a persevering love.

Love leaves no room for giving up on each other.

More Or Les

Love never fails.   — 1 Corinthians 13:8a

They met in college — Houghton College, to be exact (a most excellent Christian college if I do say so, myself). It was there that Les and Trudy fell head-over-heels in love and got married right after graduation. They began their careers as teachers and it wasn't long before the first of three beautiful boys would arrive. Trudy eventually became the principal of the Christian school where they both worked. In addition to raising the children and working full time, Les and Trudy were also both actively involved in their church. Trudy worked with the children, and Les directed the choir, in addition to all the regular services they attended. In short, Les and Trudy were actively involved in life, and life was good! In fact, they had all of the ingredients for a "happily-ever-after" kind of life together. That was, until the day Trudy went to the doctor after experiencing some odd symptoms and was diagnosed with multiple sclerosis (MS). From that point on, things would never be the same for Les and Trudy again.

Multiple sclerosis is a disease that attacks the central nervous system — the brain and the spinal cord. People with MS may experience problems with balance, muscle coordination, vision, speech, thinking, or other physical and mental abilities. The most common characteristics include fatigue, weakness, spasticity, balance problems, numbness, vision loss, tremor, and vertigo. Most people with MS begin with relapsing/remitting (RRMS) where they go through temporary periods when symptoms get worse. These periods are called relapses or attacks and typically last a few weeks. Approximately ten years after onset, about 50% of people with

RRMS will slowly pass into a secondary progressive (SPMS) phase of the disease. This is characterized by a gradual worsening of the disease between relapses. In the early phases of SPMS, people may experience good and bad days or weeks, but symptoms become steadily progressive until there are no longer any periods of complete remission and no real recovery.

After getting over the initial shock, Les and Trudy tried to just get on with their lives. After all, they knew their lives were in God's hands. They would somehow deal with this and believed with all their hearts that God would give them the grace sufficient for whatever the future held for them and their boys. At first nothing changed. They both continued to work at school and be involved at church, and the boys continued to take part in all the normal activities boys love to do. But eventually, Trudy's health started to deteriorate. At first it was a limp and trouble keeping her balance. She began to use a cane. Eventually, she lost muscle control in her legs and began to use a wheelchair to get around. At that point, it became necessary for Trudy to retire from the school after working for sixteen years. But through it all, they almost never missed a service or activity at church. And they never once complained. In fact, one could pretty much count on either Les or Trudy being one of the first to offer a word of thanks for something during praise time. Yes, they knew sickness, but they also knew the joy of the Lord and never stopped living it.

Over the next seventeen years, Les had to stand by and helplessly watch as his once-active wife, and the mother of his children, gradually progressed into SPMS. Actually, that's not true. Les never once just stood by. He was there at Trudy's side every step of the way doing whatever he could to help. As things got worse and Trudy became increasingly unable to care for herself, Les seemed to just seamlessly take over the responsibilities. When it came to the point she had to be in a special wheelchair with head support, Les bought a handicap accessible van and they continued to show up together for every church function.

Over the years, another woman in our church was diagnosed with MS. But there was one major difference. Joe ultimately left

Kathy.* Unlike Les, Joe couldn't handle watching his wife decline before his eyes, much less take on the task of caring for her physical needs. Actually, no one really knows what ultimately caused him to leave his wife at the time she needed him the most. God knows. And God, of course, is willing to forgive Joe (though, I think at the same time he left Kathy, he turned his back on God, too). But the point of mentioning him is because Joe's response is not all that uncommon. In fact, marriages fall apart over issues a lot less serious than MS. What is uncommon, is the kind of Christlike love and faithfulness Les showed to Trudy throughout her illness.

It eventually reached the point where Trudy was totally helpless. And when it did, Les took over total responsibility for all her needs. He dressed her, fed her, and cared for her as he would his own body. Just as the Bible tells us to: "Husbands, love your wives, just as Christ also loved the church and gave himself up for her ... So husbands ought also to love their own wives as their own bodies. He who loves his own wife loves himself" (Ephesians 5:25-28). Les was a living example of these words. And as far as I can remember, except for the few times Trudy was in the hospital, the two of them never missed a church service together.

The day eventually came when Trudy just quietly parted this earth and went on ahead leaving Les, and her wheelchair, behind (she has no need for it anymore). If you asked Les how he could so faithfully care for his wife even as he watched her slowly die, he would probably ask you how he could *not* do it. Trudy was his beloved wife and his best friend, the mother of their three sons, and she would have done the same for him, if things had been reversed. It's just what love is all about. It never fails. Just like God. After all, God is love.

Of course, no one's love story is over just because they die. But Les' story has a particularly interesting twist to it, even before its earthly end. One of Les' now fully grown sons started dating a young woman from church. They eventually ended up getting married. The young woman's mom, Joan, now a single mom herself, had also been a member of the church for a number of years. Planning a wedding together sort of "forced" Joan and Les to spend a

lot of time together. One day they decided to go to a church-related function together. It was pouring rain as he drove her home (she had parked her car at his home). Now, any good Christian man doesn't bring a single lady into his house late at night, so they just stood there, in the pouring rain, talking for over an hour. As Les was trying to dry himself off later that night, he wondered what in the world was going on between them (middle-aged adults don't stand in the rain in the middle of the night just to finish a conversation). Joan admits she had started to have feelings much earlier for Les, but had not told a single soul except the Lord. When Les called her the next day and said, "We need to talk!" she invited him over not knowing what was on his heart. Apparently, it was her. They were married less than a month later.

Love is faithful to the end — so is God.

* These are not their real names. I have given them new names.

Sight Unseen

But where there are prophecies, they will cease.
— 1 Corinthians 13:8b

It has always been one of my all-time favorite love stories. It's also one of the original examples of love at first sight (I think Adam and Eve get first dibs on that). It is a romantic adventure better than *Romeo And Juliet*, *Cinderella*, *Sleeping Beauty*, and *Gone With The Wind*, and it's better than all of them because it's true. And this wonderful love story all began with a prophecy.

We last left Abraham and Sarah laughing with joy over their newborn son, Isaac, whose name means, "he laughs." Sarah has now passed away and Abraham is also nearing the end of his life. Life had been good. Actually, it had been extraordinary, but one thing Abraham had been looking for had not yet come to fruition. God had prophesied that Abraham's own flesh and blood decedents would fill the land — the promised land he had taken Abraham to. But, there was even more. Because Abraham had been obedient to God, even to the point of being willing to give up his only son, Isaac, God promised Abraham that not only would he be father of a mighty nation but that "in your seed all the nations of the earth shall be blessed, because you have obeyed my voice" (Genesis 22:18).

Now, this father-to-be of many nations probably didn't fully understand all of what that promise entailed, but he did figure out that it would begin with Isaac and that Isaac needed a wife. Not just any wife, she needed to be someone who was a faithful follower of Abraham's God-of-the-promise. He also realized he would not find such a woman for Isaac there in Canaan. She would need

to come from his home country, yet be willing to relocate to the land God had promised to Abraham's descendants. So, Abraham asked his faithful servant to go back to the land of Ur and to his relatives to find Isaac a wife and bring her back to Canaan. With the same kind of faith it had taken for him to lay Isaac on the altar, Abraham was confident that, since this was God's prophecy, God would somehow provide.

The servant took ten camels, lots of goodies, and headed off to Abraham's hometown, Nahor. He arrived, tired and thirsty, at the city well and said a little prayer. Actually, some might even call it a fleece. He asked that the Lord would lead him to the right woman for Isaac and that he would confirm this by having her offer to not only give him (a complete stranger) a drink but water his ten camels, as well. Now that's a fleece. God honored the servant's bold faith and even before he finished his prayer, a beautiful young woman arrived at the well. Just as he had prayed, she gave him a drink and then said, "I will draw also for your camels until they have finished drinking" (Genesis 24:19). Almost too shocked to believe it could be true, the servant asked whose daughter she was. When he found out she was, in fact, related to Abraham, the servant fell down before the Lord and worshiped him.

The young woman, whose name was Rebekah, invited the stranger home and introduced him to her brother, Laban, and her father, Bethuel. He told them about how God had led him to her in answer to his prayer and then asked if they would allow Rebekah to be Isaac's wife. They readily agreed saying, "The matter comes from the Lord ... Behold, Rebekah is before you, take her and go, and let her be the wife of your master's son, as the Lord has spoken" (Genesis 24:50-51). Now, there was just one little glitch. As is customary, they wanted the servant to stay with them for a while and not take Rebekah right away. Knowing his master was waiting, the servant pleaded with them to let her leave with him immediately. They left it up to Rebekah to decide whether to stay there with her family and everyone she had ever known and loved, or to go off to a foreign land with a complete stranger to marry a man she had never met. Her response was immediate: "I will go." A

short time later, the servant, the ten well-watered camels, and Rebekah were all headed back to Canaan. The next question, of course, would be whether Isaac would be as excited about all of this as the servant was. I'm sure these thoughts were going through his mind as he neared Abraham's land. Here's what took place:

> *Isaac went out to meditate in the field toward evening; and he lifted up his eyes and looked, and behold, camels were coming. And Rebekah lifted up her eyes, and when she saw Isaac she dismounted from the camel. And she said to the servant, "Who is that man walking in the field to meet us?" And the servant said, "He is my master." Then she took her veil and covered herself. And the servant told Isaac all the things that he had done. Then Isaac brought her into his mother Sarah's tent, and he took Rebekah, and she became his wife; and he loved her.* — Genesis 24:62-67

It is interesting that Isaac was meditating as the caravan arrived. Was he perhaps praying for a wife? We'll never know for sure. What we do know is that it was love at first sight. We also know that Isaac was not only a praying man, but a man who prayed for his wife. Some time later we read, "Isaac prayed to the Lord on behalf of his wife, because she was barren; and the Lord answered him and Rebekah his wife conceived" (Genesis 25:21). In fact, she conceived twins, and even while they were yet in her womb, the Lord prophesied that these two sons, Esau and Jacob, would become two mighty nations and that through one of them, the younger, all of the nations would one day be blessed. God eventually changed Jacob's name to Israel, through Israel came the Messiah, and through him, God's prophecy was fulfilled. For because of Jesus, the Messiah, all nations — Jews, Gentiles, male, female, black, white, young, and old — all who put their faith in him, have been blessed. Talk about a love story with a happy ending.

Throughout their lives, Isaac and Rebekah took God at his word and trusted him to fulfill all of his promises to them even when

they were still sight unseen. For Rebekah, that meant saying, "I will go" even when she had no idea what that might require of her. And for Isaac it meant praying — boldly asking God — for that which he had prophesied — decedents through whom the entire world would be blessed. The Love Chapter states that prophecies will one day cease. Isaac and Rebekah saw the beginning of, and played an active part in, God's prophecy to bless all of the earth. The day will come when this prophecy will be fulfilled in its entirety. We will no longer be awaiting future blessings for the ultimate blessing, himself, will have come to take us to be with him. Okay, so perhaps the story of Isaac and Rebekah is my second favorite love story. The story of God's redemptive love culminating in the marriage of the Lamb to his bride, the church, is the ultimate love story. And it all began with a prophecy.

**Love believes God keeps his promises
and will bless those who are faithful to him.**

Truth Be Told ...

Where there are tongues, they will be stilled.
— 1 Corinthians 13:8c

As I was studying some of the couples in the Bible, I found a few examples that I initially wouldn't have considered as candidates for a book on marriage. As I thought about it, though, I realized everything God revealed to us through the Bible is illustrative, even if it is more of a "how not to" in some cases.

Take Samson and Delilah, for example. I'm not sure they were even married. Nevertheless, Samson fell in love with Delilah, and she (a pagan Philistine) took advantage of his love to gain information from him (that his uncut hair was the secret of his great strength). She gave it to his enemies who used it to destroy him. In other words, she betrayed his trust in her and used it against him. We can learn a lot from this tragic love story. First, if your wife wants to know who your barber is, don't tell her. More importantly, we should never use the intimate knowledge that we have of each other in our marriages to hurt or betray our partner's trust, but only to build each other up.

Another couple we can learn a few "how not to" pointers from are Ahab and Jezebel. They were definitely married, but it was definitely a marriage that should have never taken place. Ahab was king of Israel. Jezebel was the daughter of a pagan king. As soon as they were married, Jezebel had Ahab worshiping Baal with her. She later convinced Ahab to kill a man for his vineyard. She also talked him into having all of God's prophets killed (God intervened and had Jezebel's prophets killed instead). The scriptures tell us, "There was none who sold himself to do what was evil in the sight

of the Lord like Ahab, whom Jezebel his wife incited" (1 Kings 21:25). But, God is not mocked. You might say things eventually went to the dogs for this couple. In fact, we are told that dogs licked up the blood of Ahab and Jezebel after their violent deaths. Again, there are several take-home points from their story. First, they demonstrate why God has told us, "Do not be unequally yoked with unbelievers" (2 Corinthians 6:14). His intent is for us to glorify and serve him together as a couple. If you are already married to an unbeliever, don't lose heart. The Bible has some encouraging words about how your godly life and prayers can help lead your partner to Christ. (See 1 Corinthians 7:12-15 and 1 Peter 3:1-2.) The story also shows us how powerful an influence we can have on our spouses — for good or for bad. What an awesome responsibility and privilege that is. By God's grace we can play a role in helping our partners become all God intended them to be. Or, we can use our influence to ensure that our marriages go to the dogs.

Now, there's one more couple who fits the "how not to" category of marriages found in the scriptures. It was just after Christ had returned to heaven and the Holy Spirit had come upon the new believers with power. People were coming to the Lord by the thousands. The Spirit was revealing his presence in the church through signs, wonders, and miracles. The exuberant new disciples were joyfully laying their material gifts and money at the apostles' feet to help support the spreading of the gospel and to help the needy among them. Ananias and Sapphira were right there alongside the others taking in the marvels happening all around them. They, too, wanted to get involved and give of what they had. There was just one little problem in how they did it. They lied. In fact, they lied to God.

Ananias and Sapphira sold a piece of their property and then, in a public display of generosity, Ananias came to lay the money at the apostles' feet. However, instead of turning in all the money, Ananias only gave a portion, saving the rest of it for their retirement fund (which they weren't going to be needing). Peter realized what Ananias had done and confronted him saying, "Ananias, why has Satan filled your heart to lie to the Holy Spirit, and to keep

back some of the price of the land? ... You have not lied to men, but to God" (Acts 5:3-4). Ananias immediately fell down dead, was carried out and buried. About three hours later, Sapphira arrived, unaware of what had taken place. Peter asked her how much they sold the land for and she lied, giving the same figure her husband had. Peter responded, "How is it that you have agreed together to put the Spirit of the Lord to the test?" (Acts 5:9 NRSV). Sapphira, too, fell to the ground dead.

Now, remember, the outpouring of the Holy Spirit had just taken place and his newborn church was growing fast. The new believers were using their spiritual gifts, and manifesting his presence in their lives. This even included speaking in other languages. Ananias and Sapphira were probably among those who had experienced this manifestation of the Spirit. But instead of using their tongues to praise and glorify God, they used them, instead, to lie. They had plotted together as a couple to appear more generous than they actually were in the eyes of others. They had attempted to use the gifts God had given them, their possessions, and their speech, to their own glory. It cost them their lives. They say that "the couple who prays together stays together." In the case of Ananias and Sapphira, you could say that "the couple who lies together, dies together." Their deaths might seem rather harsh for what some would consider nothing more than a "white" lie. (Who decided lies can be color-coded?) This shows us that God takes sin seriously. He has called us to be holy, as individuals and as couples.

The three "how not to" couples described above remind us that God wants us to use our knowledge, our influence, and our words to build each other up and to glorify him. The Love Chapter states that "where there are tongues, they will be stilled." There won't be any unknown languages once we are standing before the throne of grace. We will all be speaking the universal language of love. And we can practice this language right now in our marriages. Unlike Ananias and Sapphira, we are told, "Instead, speaking the truth in love, we will in all things grow up into him who is the head, that is, Christ. From him the whole body ... grows and builds itself up in

love" (Ephesians 4:15-16). It should be noted that if you have experienced some "how not to" in your own marriage (who hasn't?), the final point of these stories, and the beauty of the gospel is that our God is the God of love, forgiveness, and grace. We are told, "These things happened to them as examples and were written down as warnings for us, on whom the fulfillment of the ages has come ... No temptation has seized you except what is common to man. And God is faithful; he will not let you be tempted beyond what you can bear. But when you are tempted, he will also provide a way out so that you can stand up under it" (1 Corinthians 10:11, 13). Couples who commit their marriage to Christ can be victorious examples of "how to" to the world because "the one who calls you is faithful and he will do it" (1 Thessalonians 5:24).

**Love believes God will not bless
those who are unfaithful to him.**

Personality Plus And Minus

Where there is knowledge, it will pass away.
— 1 Corinthians 13:9

I was first introduced to the "four temperaments" when I was only about twelve years old. My mom had purchased a book by O. Hallesby titled, *Temperament and the Christian Faith.* She also had a copy of a forty-question personality test you could take to discover what your temperament was. I never heard whether I passed or failed, but when she gave it to me, I did find out that I was a melancholic (with just a hint of sanguine). I wasn't even sure what the terms meant at the time, but was, nevertheless, immediately hooked. I made all my friends take the quiz and let them know what their temperament was (this is a tendency of us melancholics). Now, if you happen to be one of those "don't-even-think-about-analyzing-me" types (which tells me what temperament you are), hang in there for just a bit. It won't be painful at all, I promise, and might even help you better understand your "why-is-she-always-trying-to-analyze-me" wife (or husband).

The theory of the four temperaments is nothing new. In fact, it dates as far back as 400 BC, when the doctor and philosopher, Hippocrates, proposed that there were four fundamental personality types. He based his theory on the mistaken idea that these four types were the result of different bodily liquids. Hence, he referred to them as sanguine (blood), choleric (from choler or yellow bile), melancholy (black bile), and phlegmatic (phelgm).

Perhaps a little more detailed description of each would be helpful. The sanguine personality is the outgoing, fun-loving, life of the party. She is warm, lively, and cheerful. She loves to be around

people and is extremely likeable. She is very much in touch with her emotions (as is everyone around her) and relates well to others. She generally doesn't like spending time alone. She is a natural salesperson or actress and when she enters a room, she rarely goes unnoticed.

The choleric is the hard-driving achiever. He is goal-oriented and strong-willed. I read one description that called him irascible, but I didn't know what that word meant so, let's just call him a potential hothead. But when his temper is under control, he is the one who gets things done. He is self-directed, decisive, and is a natural leader though some might feel a bit walked over when he has set his mind on reaching a goal. Yet, in the Lord's hands, this is the person who will be able to accomplish great things for God.

The melancholic (I'll try not to be biased), is bright, creative, artistic, and neat, but can also be gloomy and negative. She is creative, analytical, and detail-oriented. This can lead her, at times, to being a perfectionist who can be critical and who dwells on flaws in herself and others. She tends to be moody and introverted. She is often an inventor, artist, composer, or philosopher. She is slow to make friends, but once she does, she will be a loyal and self-sacrificing friend for life.

The phlegmatic is easy-going, unexcitable, slow-moving, and sometimes timid. He is calm and pleasant to be around, is laid back, and is easy to get along with. That coupled with his dry sense of humor explains why he often has so many friends. He will not volunteer for a leadership position but if he can be prodded into accepting, makes an excellent leader. He is a natural peacemaker but tends to be late and doesn't always get around to things he knows he needs to do.

Assuming that at least all of the melancholic and sanguine readers are now intrigued enough to take a temperament test of their own, I've included a few links to online quizzes at the end of this chapter, along with a couple of my favorite books on this subject in case you would like to explore this further. Just don't be blaming me if your spouse comes after you with forty questions.

Since each of us is a unique individual, we are usually a blend of several of these different personality types. Having an understanding of the various temperaments can help couples work through some of their differences. It also enables them understand why they respond to each other in such different ways. It also lends truth to that old expression, "Opposites attract." We do tend to be attracted to those with complimentary strengths. Interestingly, some of those very characteristics and strengths that first attract us to each other often end up being the very traits that cause us the most conflict in our marriages. That's because, being fallen and imperfect beings and all, our strengths have corresponding weaknesses. That bubbly, outgoing girl you married, for example, just might end up seeming like an incessant chatterbox who wants to throw a party every night of the week. And that deep, introspective philosopher you married, can tend to be moody or even downright morbid at times.

I'm not suggesting that we should all marry someone just like ourselves. In fact, quite the opposite. It is precisely because we have different areas of strength and weakness that we need or complement each other. Understanding that we were each created with a unique combination of personality traits, helps us learn to accept our differences, to appreciate each others strengths, to be aware of our own individual weaknesses, and by the power of the Holy Spirit living in us, to allow him to transform us into his image. The Lord can take our natural weaknesses (let's just be honest here — some of our "weaknesses" are just plain old sinfulness) and turn them into strengths that bring glory to himself.

For example, that procrastinating, never-get-the-family-to-church-on-time guy, under the power of the Spirit, can become the elder at church that everyone comes to for help, including his family, because of his calm and gentle spirit. That dictator dad who spends more time driving a hard bargain at work than driving his kids to a soccer match can become the Spirit-filled father who organizes the neighborhood little league. In God's hands, it is all possible.

One of the greatest advantages in learning about the temperaments is that it helped me acknowledge my own weaknesses (okay,

sins) and turn them over to the Lord, allowing him to begin transforming them into strengths. When we allow the Spirit to do his wondrous work in our lives, he can turn some of our worst natural tendencies into Spirit-filled attributes that glorify him. It also can't help but to make our marriages stronger.

Now, I truly believe that understanding temperaments can be very helpful in relating to our spouses and in coming to understand why we relate to each other in such different ways. A little knowledge can go a long way in learning to work through our differences. But, all that said, it can't take us the whole way. As the Love Chapter puts it, "knowledge will pass away." There will be times when, no matter how many tests, how much theoretical understanding we have, it won't be enough to face the conflicts and disagreements couples encounter. That's where love kicks in. On the bad days, it is not knowledge but love — specifically the love of God — that can turn our confrontations into celebrations. When we surrender our conflicts to the one who dwells in our hearts, he will invade our marriages with power and bring us victory Hippocrates never even dreamed of. Though, Hippocrates might have gotten some mileage out of his liquid theory. Jesus said, "Indeed, the water I give him will become in him a spring of water welling up to eternal life" (John 4:14). Filled with the Spirit, no matter what our temperament, we can live lives and have marriages that glorify God.

**Love seeks to understand
but continues to love when it can't.**

Online Temperament Quizzes
http://weddingplannerandguide.com/plan_profiletest.php
http://www.oneishy.com/personality/personality_test.php

Web Articles
http://www.ylcf.org/you/personality.htm (YLCF)
http://www.veritaschristi.org/articles/family_spirituality/2005/
temperment.htm (T.G. Morrow)

Books
Florence Littauer. *Personality Plus*, Revell, div. of Baker Books, 1992.

Tim LaHaye. *Spirit-Controlled Temperament*, Tyndale House, 1971.

O. Hallesby. *Temperament and the Christian Faith*, Augsburg Publishing House, 1962.

Gift Baskets

For we know in part and we prophesy in part, but when
perfection comes, the imperfect disappears.
— 1 Corinthians 13:10

As much as I have always enjoyed studying (and quizzing all my friends) about the various types of temperaments we have, I realize that God has given each of his children something far more important yet just as individualized. When we come to Christ, one of the countless blessings he bestows upon us are spiritual gifts — gifts that will enable each of us to serve him in our own unique way. I was, of course, aware that these gifts existed but when someone introduced me to a quiz I could take ... (oh no, here she goes again) ... let me just say that it got me really excited about the whole thing! I suppose the quiz helped me realize we can identify areas where God has specially enabled us to help others, both inside and outside of the church. Each of us were custom designed, not just to fit in, but to have an active and effective role in the body of Christ. And, before you ask, yes, I will include links to some online spiritual gift tests at the end of this chapter just in case you'd like to take one, too. Though, do keep in mind that any lists of the spiritual gifts God bestows upon his children are not exhaustive. God's gifts are limitless so lists are merely representative of some of the ways he chooses to gift individuals. Plus, each of us may and often do have more than one spiritual gift in combination, and in varying degrees. The gifts the Spirit gives are custom designed just like we are. So, even in taking a quiz, the point isn't to nail down a particular formula or label, but only to help you identify some of the unique ways God has gifted you to help his body grow and to glorify him.

Is all of this biblical, you ask? Admittedly, much more so than the four temperaments. But, that said, here are a few of the spiritual gifts identified in the Bible: administration, discernment, evangelism, exhortation, faith, giving, healing, helps, hospitality, intercession, interpretation, knowledge, leadership, mercy, miracles, prophecy, serving, shepherding, teaching, tongues, wisdom. In addition, many feel the Bible also includes the following as spiritual gifts: pastor, apostle, evangelist, missionary, musician, craftsman.

Though the use of spiritual gifts is found throughout the scriptures, there are three places that very specifically state each of us have been given spiritual gifts and identifies them. In Romans we read,

> *We have different gifts, according to the grace given us. If a man's gift is prophesying, let him use it in proportion to his faith. If it is serving, let him serve; if it is teaching, let him teach; if it is encouraging, let him encourage; if it is contributing to the needs of others, let him give generously; if it is leadership, let him govern diligently; if it is showing mercy, let him do it cheerfully ... Be joyful in hope, patient in affliction, faithful in prayer. Share with God's people who are in need. Practice hospitality.* — Romans 12:6-13

In Paul's letter to the church at Corinth he writes,

> *Now to each one the manifestation of the Spirit is given for the common good. To one there is given through the Spirit the message of wisdom, to another the message of knowledge by means of the same Spirit, to another faith by the same Spirit, to another gifts of healing by that one Spirit, to another miraculous powers, to another prophecy, to another distinguishing between spirits, to another speaking in different kinds of tongues, and to still another the interpretation of tongues. All these are the work of one and the same Spirit, and he gives them to each one, just as he determines.* — 1 Corinthians 12:7-11

And finally, to the Ephesians he wrote,

This is why it says: "When he ascended on high, he led captives in his train and gave gifts to men." ... It was he who gave some to be apostles, some to be prophets, some to be evangelists, and some to be pastors and teachers, to prepare God's people for works of service, so that the body of Christ may be built up.
— Ephesians 4:8, 11-12

It is important to note that in each of these passages Paul went on to give some very specific instructions and guidelines about how (and how not) to put our spiritual gifts to use. As with any good gift, the potential to misuse them has been around for just about as long as the gifts, themselves.

Now, how does this relate to us as couples? How can understanding our own spiritual gifts and those of our spouses make a difference in our marriages, our families, our churches, and our world? Or, did I just bring this stuff up to make you take another online quiz?

God has given us spiritual gifts for the purpose, as Paul explained, of building up the body. As couples, he has also given us as gifts to each other for the same purpose. God has put us together, with our unique combination of spiritual gifts, to build each other up. We can also use our complimentary spiritual gifts as couples in synergy to minister to others. If we surrender ourselves, our marriages, and the gifts God has given us to him, we can accomplish ... well, let me put it this way: When the New Testament Spirit-filled believers worked together, using the gifts God had given them, even the nonbelievers who observed them exclaimed, "These ... have turned the world upside down" (Acts 17:6 KJV). He is the same Spirit and these are the same gifts we've been given today so, as married couples, why expect anything less? God can turn the world upside down through couples who have dedicated their lives to serving him together. So, it might not be all that bad an idea to take one of those online quizzes after all. Sit down together, and

assess the various gifts God has given you. Come before him in prayer and dedicate the gifts each of you have been given to him. Seek his direction as to how you, as a team, might be able to put your gifts to use. Then just watch and see what wonderful things the Lord can do through the two of you working together.

It is interesting that the chapter immediately following one of the passages on the spiritual gifts is the Love Chapter. In fact, the Love Chapter itself mentions the spiritual gifts in several places. In the first, we are told that even if we were to have every gift (prophecy, tongues, knowledge, giving, and the like) but didn't have love, our gifts would be completely useless. Gifts are good; love is better. Gifts are both temporary and incomplete; love is eternal and perfect. We are told, "For we know in part and we prophesy in part, but when perfection comes, the imperfect disappears." You see, love is not a spiritual gift that some have and others don't. It is a spiritual fruit that is ours for the asking because the Spirit of love is already dwelling in our hearts. We are told to, "live by the Spirit, and you will not gratify the desires of the sinful nature" (Galatians 5:16) and that "the fruit of the Spirit is love, joy, peace, patience, kindness, goodness, faithfulness, gentleness and self-control" (Galatians 5:22-23).

Couples who are filled with the fruit of the Spirit, can use the gifts of the Spirit synergistically to accomplish great things for the kingdom of God. Working together as a Spirit-filled team, we can take all those gifts, and all that fruit, and create some very lovely gift baskets.

Love uses its gifts in synchrony to serve the Lord together.

Online Spiritual Gift Tests

http://www.churchgrowth.org/analysis/index.html

http://www.buildingchurch.net/g2s.htm (also with some great follow-up for further study)

http://www.christianet.com/bible/spiritualgiftstest.htm (a shorter one for impatient cholerics)

Burnt Offerings

When I was a child, I spoke like a child, I thought like a child, I reasoned like a child. — 1 Corinthians 13:11a

Sometimes it's not as important how a loving gesture turns out, as the thought behind the gesture. However, one would have to ask Barb whether that concept has universal application. Barb was well along in her pregnancy and was just plain worn out. This being their first child, Brian wanted to do everything he could (short of carrying the baby himself) to make things a little easier for her. Having to cook dinner for them at the end of a tiring day was one of the most difficult tasks (or so he reasoned) that she had to do. So, despite the fact that he had no experience in cooking, he assumed the expression "true love conquers all" could easily be applied to the culinary arts. He sent his weary but dubious bride off to bed. Then, the household hunter-gatherer headed off to the kitchen to valiantly do battle and, with any luck, victoriously return to her with the proverbial fatted calf.

Being a very honest person, Brian had warned his wife that he was totally inept in all things kitchen (thus explaining her being dubious). Even having admitted as much, as he stood in the middle of this strange and hostile land, he still surprised himself at how little he really did know. After a rather long period of silence, Barb called downstairs to see if everything was okay, and if there was anything she could do to help. Brian assured her that everything was under control (at that point everything still was) but having been given the invitation, he started making frequent flights up and down the stairs asking her questions as he thought of them (the

evening ended up being a very fine aerobic workout for him by the time it was all said and done).

Once Brian had figured out the lay of the land, and had the menu planned, he assumed that the rest was really going to be quite easy. He took the potpie out of the freezer (that was the menu, by the way), successfully opened the box, put it on "the metal thing inside the oven" (also known to some as the rack), and "let it rip" (also known as turning on the oven). Having taken dominion over the situation, an exhausted Brian triumphantly sat down on the couch to await the anticipated feast. *Yes, true love conquers all*, he proudly thought to himself.

As he was daydreaming about what exciting cuisine he might come up with for tomorrow's meal, he began to realize that something coming from approximately the same direction as the kitchen smelled like it was burning. Unfortunately, Barb had come to the same realization just a little bit before Brian did. She jumped out of bed and ran down the stairs to see what the problem was. She threw open the oven door and a cloud of dark smoke billowed out into the kitchen. Apparently, the directions on the box had not specified which direction on a potpie was up. Brian had placed the potpie upside down in the oven! When telling the story, to this day he stands by his conviction that it looked right to him at the time but does concede, "I guess it really does make a difference. It was more like a burnt offering." Apparently, Barb agreed. That happened over twenty years ago and she has not asked Brian for any help with dinner ever since.

Indeed, one would have to wonder whether it really is the thought behind the gesture that counts most. Brian's heroic efforts on Barb's behalf obviously didn't contribute much to the rest Barb needed. But, if you asked her, Barb would say Brian's burnt offering meant the world to her. In the Bible, we read, "when I was a child, I spoke like a child...." In other words, children speak like children. We expect that of them. And inept cooks cook like inept cooks. Or at least they did in Brian's case. It is quite likely that their unborn baby could have done a better job preparing dinner than Brian. But inept in the kitchen or not, his brave attempt at

providing for his family did not go unnoticed, not just because he nearly burned the house down, but because it was done out of his love for his wife. Yes, sometimes our best attempts at "helping" each other will actually make things worse. Yet, these faltering expressions of love are often the most powerful statements we can make. Much like that one-eyed monster drawing your child hands you and says, "Look mommie! I drew your picture." Through the eyes of love, it is a masterpiece. So is the burnt offering prepared by the hands of love. What might be clumsy at best and an absolute disaster at worst, shows our willingness to sacrificially put the needs of our partner before our own. It also shows a humble servant-like attitude that is not too proud to "mess up" if that's what it takes to minister to our spouse. Truth be told, doing things we are uncomfortable with can end up being very humbling ... in fact, downright humiliating. But it fulfills God's mandate to "be devoted to one another in brotherly love. Honor one another above yourselves. Never be lacking in zeal, but keep your spiritual fervor, serving the Lord" (Romans 12:9-11). When we minister to the needs of our spouses, we are also serving the Lord.

Now, for the one on the receiving end of one of these humbling gestures of love, it is important to remember that the one being "served" has some responsibilities as well. How important it is, when one partner makes a valiant attempt to help the other, that we never criticize or condemn even the most disastrous of outcomes. Little can dampen any expression of love more than belittling or ridicule no matter how burnt the offering. We are told, "Now we who are strong ought to bear the weaknesses of those without strength and not just please ourselves" (Romans 15:1). So, whether we are the giver or the receiver, whether the outcome is grandly successful or a near death experience, we need to keep Christ's own example to us in mind:

> *Do nothing out of selfish ambition or vain conceit, but in humility consider others better than yourselves. Each of you should look not only to your own interests, but also to the interests of others. Your attitude should be*

the same as that of Christ Jesus: Who, being in very nature God, did not consider equality with God something to be grasped, but made himself nothing, taking the very nature of a servant, being made in human likeness. And being found in appearance as a man, he humbled himself and became obedient to death — even death on a cross!   — Philippians 2:3-8

And he did it all because he loves us. That much!

Getting back to Brian, perhaps I'm being extra generous because Bob has had to experience so many of my own burnt offerings, but I think I can honestly speak for any spouse whose partner has made a wholehearted attempt to leave his or her comfort zone, to boldly go where no man (or woman) has gone before. When the driving motivation is love, it really is the thought that counts.

**Love is giving your best
even when you aren't sure how.**

Give Me A Brake!

When I became a man, I put childish ways behind me.
— 1 Corinthians 13:11b

If one were able to look back in time, to the first few years of some of the couples who are happily married today, one might be surprised to discover what humble beginnings they had. Maybe I've grown skeptical in my old ... er ... maturing age, but I don't think anyone, no matter how perfect their relationship may seem at this point, could honestly say they never went through a few bumps along the way, even if they eventually arrived at a state of marital bliss. Perhaps "growing pains" are a more accurate way to put it.

When I asked Wes to share some favorite moments from his fifty plus years of marriage with Mary Beth, I suppose I was thinking of roses and chocolates, or breakfast in bed, or something along those lines. Isn't that the stuff people love to hear about? Or perhaps even a chivalrous rescue reminiscent of Harvey and Flo's bat attack. What came to his mind, if nothing else, gives us a more realistic glimpse at some of those first faltering years of learning to relate to one another. Lest anyone has found themselves in a similar situation and thought they were unique, or that there was something severely wrong with their marriage, it might come as an encouragement to hear how Wes and Mary Beth left the marital starting gate over fifty years ago.

Mary Beth and I had been married while we were still in college and we enjoyed being poor along with all of our married classmates.

113

One afternoon I persuaded my wife to take me downtown to a sporting goods store where they had a fantastic deal on starter's clubs for golfers. She reminded me that we did not include the golf clubs in our budget, but I made big promises of what I would give up for the next 25 years if she would only consent this one time to my extravagance. As she was driving toward town, we agreed that I would not be long in the store so that she would only have to drive around the block and then pick me up. I jumped out of the car and walked into the store, made my purchase, and with great enthusiasm went outside to wait for her by the curb. She didn't come and she didn't come. I began to think the worst, that she had an accident or even something more awful like being kidnapped. I was going to start to walk around the block when I heard her voice calling me. I turned and saw her walking as fast as she could toward me.

Between tears she told me that as I soon as I got out of the car and walked inside she drove to the corner and prepared to make a right hand turn. Instead she heard a loud screeching noise and she could hardly turn the steering wheel. Fighting with the wheels and hearing this screech told her that something serious had happened to the car. Only half a block away was an automobile dealer and she managed to arrive there with the entire population staring at her. Once inside, they calmed her down but told her she would need new brakes and perhaps other parts. How much would it cost? The estimate was $75 to $100. Mary Beth broke down in tears and the service manager tried his best to assure her that he would charge the least amount he could.

We stood in front of the sporting goods store, her crying and telling me to take back the golf clubs while I held on tightly to the box and telling her I would find the money to pay for them both. This was the time for me to take on the responsibility for our financial well being even though I had never written the first check, made the first deposit, or knew where the bank was that housed our fortune. Mary Beth was so angry that she began the walk home. I trailed her and tried to comfort her but to no avail. Finally, I tried to joke with her and ask her if she would carry the golf clubs for a

short distance since I was growing tired. I had never seen that look from her before or since in our fifty years of marriage.

Probably just as well. Too many of those looks and there might not have been fifty years of marriage. I laughed when I heard Wes' fond memories of their earliest days of wedded bliss. I still haven't confirmed whether this would have also been one of the memories Mary Beth would have most treasured from their first few years together.

The point of my sharing this particularly unique love story is because I think we can all learn something rather wonderful from it (Disclaimer: I am *not* endorsing any male readers to go buy golf clubs!). The reason Wes can look back at those days and laugh about it is because he and Mary Beth are still together fifty years later (I forgot to ask if he still has the golf clubs). They were somehow able to turn this little incident into an adventure that ultimately drew them closer. Of course, it wouldn't have had to. In today's world, Wes' libertarian approach to their finances could have been considered a clear case for divorce. Asking your wife to carry the golf clubs you just purchased with the brake money would, to some, fall under the category of "irreconcilable differences." But to them, it was nothing more than an opportunity to practice evil glares and Christlike forgiveness — and to learn from their mistakes. The Love Chapter describes it as putting away childish things (what ever *did* happen to those golf clubs?). Another way to think of it is maturing. In fact, adventures like the golf club chronicles are the perfect opportunity to learn from and grow closer together. James wrote, "Consider it pure joy, my brothers, whenever you face trials of many kinds, because you know that the testing of your faith develops perseverance. Perseverance must finish its work so that you may be mature and complete, not lacking anything" (James 1:2-4). Apparently, in some cases that even includes both golf clubs and brakes.

Which reminds me — Wes added a little addendum to his fateful tale.

***

P.S. I did keep the clubs, the brakes were fixed at a minimum cost, and within months it became one of our favorite stories.

***

So, there really was a moral to this particular story. There *will* be some blunders and poor judgment being used in even the best of marriages, especially early on. What we can learn from Wes and Mary Beth, who are still happily married more than fifty years after the long walk home, is that mess-ups need never be reasons to quit. Divorce simply wasn't an option for them (murder, perhaps, but not divorce). Instead, the blunders can be seen as opportunities to "put away childish things" and sometimes even just to have a good laugh. And above all, to grow in love. As Paul put it, "Bear with each other and forgive whatever grievances you may have against one another. Forgive as the Lord forgave you. And over all these virtues put on love, which binds them all together in perfect unity" (Colossians 3:13-14).

Love learns from, and laughs at, its mistakes.

Sight For Sore Eyes

Now we see but a poor reflection as in a mirror; then we shall see face to face. — 1 Corinthians 13:12a

There are two reasons I thought that this particular chapter would be important to include in my collection of love stories. First, I figured that after telling Wes' golf club story, it might be a good idea to offer some evidence that he really did learn his lesson and go on to have a deep and loving relationship with Mary Beth (fifty years and counting). But this story is also a reminder that even in this present fallen world, we can trust that the Lord will see us through whatever difficulties we might encounter as married couples. Sometimes he does it even before we realize we are in trouble and need his help. Wes and Mary Beth never saw it coming. But God did, and he faithfully provided for them every step of the way. Let Wes explain it.

When our son was born we were told at the first pediatrician's visit that it appeared that David had cataracts. We asked the doctor if they were painful. He said, "No," but that we should see an eye doctor. We were only in our first parsonage a few days. I had graduated from seminary in the spring, accepted a call to be a mission developer, and moved to our new home. David cried a lot, so much that I thought I would never make it through the first year as a father. The only time he was somewhat quiet was when he slept against his mother's breast. David had been born several weeks premature and weighed less than four pounds. He seemed to eat

well, added some pounds, and came home after about ten days. But after we moved, his crying seemed to get worse. It was no problem for me to stay busy making house-to-house calls and announcing the formation of a new congregation. I could walk all day, write down names and addresses, and then send out notes all night. Mary Beth stayed home, took care of the house, and learned to walk with David perched on her hip. Nights sometimes were a nightmare for all three of us.

One Sunday after church, we decided to meet another couple who were also mission developers to look at some model homes being built in their community. As we were walking through the house Mary Beth asked me if I would hold David for a while. Being the proud father that I was in the presence of company, I walked toward the bathroom. Once inside the bathroom and under the artificial light I looked at my son and saw a bright red jagged circle surrounding his right eyeball. None of us had ever seen anything like it. We rushed to our friends' home and with their advice placed phone calls to several eye specialists. The first one couldn't see us because he was on his way to Russia. After another few calls, we reached a doctor who told us to bring the baby immediately to his office. Within the hour, Dr. Malachi Sloan had examined him, called the hospital, and made preparation to do surgery the next morning. He told us that he had just finished a study on congenital glaucoma with some other eye surgeons in Boston and that he would rely on their help. The next morning, Dr. Sloan performed surgery with a headset phone discussing the surgery with doctors from Boston. When we saw David for the first time after the surgery, he looked somewhat like a frog with very puffy eyes. Dr. Sloan said he would be blind in his right eye but they had saved the left eye and he would be able to do all things in a normal way. Mary Beth and I thanked God for leading us through the steps in time to save our son's eyesight and for the doctors that used God's guidance and imagination.

Even before Wes and Mary Beth knew anything was wrong God was keeping *his* eye on David, and at just the right time he provided the help they needed. Even in how Wes retold the story, it was obvious to me that he and Mary Beth went through it all with an assumed trust in the faithfulness of God. When they realized David had a problem, they did everything they could to care for their child and seek the best medical care possible. They weren't thwarted or discouraged when several doctors were unable to help them but just kept trying until they found one who was. They eventually came to see that it was only because the other doctors were unavailable, that they found the one who was prepared for this very eye problem. They knew, without a doubt, that it was God who guided their paths every step of the way. I found it interesting that the name of the doctor the Lord led them to was Malachi which, in Hebrew, means "my messenger" (or "my angel"). Wes and Mary Beth were extremely thankful that God had provided for them through the hands of this particular angel he had sent. God used Dr. Malachi Sloan to personally deliver the message of his love and faithfulness to Wes, Mary Beth, and David.

David can see today, albeit with only one eye, but he will one day see the Lord with both eyes, face-to-face. Our spiritual vision is much the same. Through his word and by his Spirit, God has given us a partial vision of himself or, as the Love Chapter puts it, "in a mirror, dimly" (NRSV). But he has promised us that one day "we shall see him as he is" (1 John 3:2). For now, we walk by faith in what God *has* revealed to us about himself. We know he is good, powerful, faithful, and kind. As Jesus told his disciples, "Anyone who has seen me has seen the Father" (John 14:9). In him, we saw love and compassion, and the God who heals. Yet, we still see a world filled with tragedy and suffering, and babies who lose an eye due to a serious illness.

Thankfully, this world is not the whole story. God has given all who are willing to look for it a glimpse of a better world that awaits those who put their trust in him. Wes and Mary Beth saw a reflection of it when God intervened and led them to the doctor who saved their son's eyesight. We also get a glimpse of it through the

love that we, as married couples, have for each other. Marriage is God's tangible demonstration to the world of the kind of relationship we will one day have with Christ, himself, when he returns to consummate his relationship with his bride, the church. And what a joyous reunion it will be. God has given us a glimpse of that, as well: "Then I heard what sounded like a great multitude ... shouting: 'Hallelujah! For our Lord God almighty reigns. Let us rejoice and be glad and give him glory! For the wedding of the Lamb has come, and his bride has made herself ready' " (Revelation 19:6-7). Or, to put it another way, "Par-ty!" We are told, "No longer will there be any curse. The throne of God and of the Lamb will be in the city, and his servants will serve him. They will see his face" (Revelation 22:3-4). Yes, we see reflections of Christ in our love for each other. We also live in anticipation of the glorious day when we will quite literally see him face-to-face.

**Love sees glimpses of God's faithfulness
even in this present fallen world.**

Listening To Love

Now I know in part; then I shall know fully, even as I am fully known. — 1 Corinthians 13:12b

Valerie went to bed early on the night of October 11, 2000. She had been struggling with a bad cold so she finally succumbed to taking a dose of liquid nighttime cold medicine, knowing it would "knock her out" for the next eight hours or longer. And as expected, she was sound asleep within minutes. Not as expected, she found herself wide awake at 4:00 in the morning. In Val's own words, here's what happened: "A little after 4 a.m., the Holy Spirit woke me up and said very clearly 'Pray for your husband!' I was in a mental fog, and started to argue 'Lord, it's four in the morning, and I'm sick. I'll pray for him when I wake up, like I always do.' The Holy Spirit was insistent. 'Pray for your husband now.' 'Okay, Lord. I guess you know what you're doing.' So I prayed this prayer: 'Lord, I don't know why you want me to pray for Tony, but I trust you. If he's about to do something he shouldn't or go somewhere he shouldn't, please stop him. Please put a hedge around my Tony, and give your angels charge over him. I ask this in Jesus' name. Amen.' I went back to sleep."

Meanwhile, across the ocean, harbored in the Yemeni port of Aden, Tony was working in his "office" space also known as combat systems maintenance central which was one of the watch stations on the naval ship where he was stationed. His friend, Chief Petty Officer Richard Costelow, was on duty with him at the time. The ship was at port for a routine fueling so there wasn't a lot going on. So, when the word, "Early dinner for watch reliefs" was given, Rich decided to head right down to the CPO mess for lunch.

There was no reason whatsoever for Tony not to go with him. Well, almost no reason. Tony explains, "I was working on one of my ongoing projects, adding all the equipment maintenance for my 'shop' to the maintenance scheduling program. I was about half-way through a stack of twelve locater cards as Rich left. I clearly remember thinking, *It's Mexican Fiesta for lunch today, that's usually pretty good.* I got as far as organizing the cards to finish the stack after lunch when out of the blue, I thought, *I really don't want to do this after lunch.* So I finished the stack of cards. As it turned out that was the difference between surviving and not surviving. Just as I finished the last card in the stack and was closing the program, the bomb went off."

Tony VanCampen had been working on the *USS Cole.* And it turned out that at the very time Val had been awakened to pray, a suicide bomber had crashed a small boat, filled with explosives, into the side of the ship right by the mess deck where the sailors were eating their lunch. Seventeen sailors were killed, including Tony's friend, Rich, and 39 others were injured in the blast. Tony was not one of them.

After getting over the initial shock, Tony realized that all of the ship's communication systems had been taken down by the blast. As he feverishly worked alongside his fellow sailors he silently prayed, "God, I don't see any way that we can communicate with the rest of the world or even the Navy. Please let Val know that I'm okay."

Meanwhile, back at home the phone woke Val up at around 8:00 that morning as the preliminary reports of the explosion started hitting the airwaves. Tony's dad had called to see if Val had heard what was going on and whether she had heard from Tony. When he told her that the bomb had hit a little after 11 a.m. Tony's time, Val immediately realized this was right when she had prayed. She wasn't afraid, at first — certain that her Tony was okay. After all, God had awakened her to pray. It was only after going to a briefing for the ship's dependents and family members and seeing the first pictures of the ship that she started to be concerned. You see, Val realized that the gaping hole in the side of the ship was right where the

mess deck formerly used to be. She also remembered that the ship started serving lunch around 11 a.m. As Val put it, "If you have ever met my Tony, you would have noticed that he is a little fluffy around the middle. He very seldom misses a meal. I was beginning to be very frightened. For eight hours I sat in a large conference room, with other spouses and parents of crew members. We wore big name tags with both our names and the names of our crew members. Some people were escorted out by counselors and military personnel. They did not return, and everyone wondered who would be next. I finally got the word that Tony was okay around 8 p.m."

God answered Val's prayer. What is even more wondrous is that it was God, himself, who put the prayer on Val's heart in the first place. In fact, through the gentle prompting of his Spirit he told her when to pray and how to pray. He even enabled her, despite the medications she was on, to be able to pray. All that was required of Val, at that point, was obedience and, of course, love. How easy it would have been to squelch the Spirit and return to sleep that fateful night in October. Thankfully, for Tony and for Val, she did not. You see, Valerie VanCampen loves Tony. She also loves God, and she knows he loves Tony even more than she ever could. Hence, she knew she could trust him when he led her to pray even when she didn't know the reasoning behind his request. When Val was awakened by the Spirit on the evening of October 11 and urged to pray for her husband, she didn't fully understand why at the time. But she knew all she needed to know at that point in time. It wasn't until the next day that she came to know fully. It is in the Love Chapter of the Bible that we read these words: "Now I know in part; then I shall know fully, even as I am fully known" (1 Corinthians 13:12b). Val knew that when God spoke, she was listening to love. She knew that this loving God was trustworthy and, hence, that Tony needed her prayers. Val was faithful to do what she knew to do and God rewarded her (and Tony, too) for her faithfulness.

The answer to prayer that Tony and Val received that October might be a little more dramatic and direct than some of us will

experience. At least in this life. Though, I tend to believe that many of our prayers are being dramatically answered in ways far beyond our earthly comprehension. Some day we may come to know fully all of what our prayers accomplished. And I have the feeling we may be surprised at some of the wondrous things taking place behind the scenes, in the heavenly realms. But for now, we can rest assured that God will reveal to us all that we need to know. If we'll trust him enough to obey his loving voice and step out in faith, he will enable us to accomplish all he has asked us to do. The rest is up to him.

In our marriages, one thing we know for sure is that we are called to love each other. How much? The Bible is clear on that. We are to love each other with the same kind of sacrificial Calvary-like love that Christ had for each of us. We are told, "Husbands, love your wives, just as Christ loved the church and gave himself up for her" (Ephesians 5:25) and that "Love must be sincere." We are told to "be devoted to one another in brotherly love. Honor one another above yourselves" (Romans 12:9-10). Just as Christ did for each of us, we are to put the needs of others, starting with our spouses, over our own. That much we know. And sometimes that's all we need to know. Sometimes that means getting up in the middle of the night to pray. At all times it means we are to be upholding each other in prayer (1 Thessalonians 5:17). If we are faithful to pray for each other and are continually listening to God's loving voice, we won't always see immediate and dramatic results. But as we fulfill all of what we know we are to do, sometimes he'll allow us a little glimpse of the "why," as he did in the case of Val and Tony. And, of course, some day we will know fully.

Love means we never stop praying for each other.

We're All Going To Die

And not these three remain: faith ...
— 1 Corinthians 13:13a

I have known Margaret and George for as long as I can remember. That is due, in part, to the fact that Margaret and George are my parents. This past year they celebrated their fifty-fifth wedding anniversary. Anyone who has remained together for 55 years has got to have something helpful to say about marriage. Having been able to observe theirs firsthand, I feel sufficiently qualified to identify a few secrets to their success.

Mom and Dad were married on July 14, 1951. At that point, neither of them had any kind of relationship with God. Dad considered himself an "agnostic" meaning, as he explains it, he just didn't know if there was a God. As for Mom, if there was a God, she simply had no interest in him. Thankfully, God had an interest in Margaret and George. Shortly after they got married they moved into their first home, right next door to Helen and Jack who were Bible-believing Christians. Thanks to Helen and Jack's bold witness and their prayers, both Mom and Dad came to not only believe in God, but to commit their lives to him.

One of the first observations one might make about Mom and Dad is that they have very different personalities (as they say, "opposites attract"). Dad is a quiet, soft-spoken man. I had figured, as a child, that must be why God gave him my mom. She is very outgoing and, in fact, enjoys engaging anyone she meets in conversation. Another area in which my parents complement each other in is in how they express their emotions. No matter what catastrophe they encountered, Dad always seemed to remain calm

and Mom ... well, she usually didn't. My favorite example from childhood was the day we were crossing a wide river in a boat. The wind suddenly cropped up and the waves got extremely rough. The boat began to take quite a pounding as we attempted to drive directly into the wind (and toward home). Dad appeared perfectly calm as he navigated the boat, while Mom stood on the back deck and announced, "We're all going to die!" I had no reason to doubt her, so I cowered in the bow with my life jacket on wondering if God might send a large fish if I promised to never disobey my parents again.

We all laugh when we think of that adventure (we didn't die, by the way), but this isn't the best example I could give of the kind of faith my mom had. The apostle Peter could probably relate to her response to the waves, and look how God eventually used him). In reality, it is that same outgoing nature and her intense emotions that have made Mom so willing to boldly share her faith and her love for the Lord with others. Countless people have heard that Jesus loves them because of my mother's God-given passion for the lost.

Mom and Dad are now in their eighties. As most eighty-year-olds, they have gone through a battery of health-related issues. Mom fell and badly broke her leg. After the operation, she was left with a limp from which she never fully recovered. Throughout the hospitalization and recovery period, Dad was there for her, being everything from chauffeur, to chef, to housekeeper, until she was well enough to get around once again.

Not long after that, Dad needed to have heart surgery. The night before the operation, Mom and I stood by his bed, each of us holding one of his hands, knowing that there was a chance he might not come through the operation. Dad told us not to worry because even if he didn't come through, he had total peace about where he was going. Mom responded by telling him that he was most definitely going to come through the operation. And that was all there was to it. After almost fifty years of marriage, Dad knew better than to argue. He would simply have to come through the operation. Thankfully, he did. The night he got home from the hospital, weak and

disoriented, Mom helped him up to bed and then proceeded to care for him day and night, despite her own medical problems, until she had lovingly nurtured him back to health.

This past year, it was Dad's turn, once again, to be caretaker. Mom fell and ended up in the hospital for almost two months. Every single day Dad came and sat by her bed. Every evening he took home her laundry, took down a list of things she needed from home, went home and cared for the house and the dog, made his own meals, did the shopping and the laundry, then returned the next day to sit, once again, by his beloved's side.

One night while I was there with them, I told them about a friend of mine who was going through a divorce over what seemed like some rather minor issues. Mom sat up in her bed, clearly distraught and said, "Well, they simply don't understand what the marriage covenant is all about." Now, in all honesty, Mom and Dad's marriage was as full of bumps, difficulties, disagreements, and disappointments as anyone else's. They could have just as easily given up on their marriage. But, as Mom put it, that's not what the marriage covenant is all about. Jesus explained it this way: "... the Creator made them male and female, and said, 'For this reason a man will leave his father and mother and be united to his wife, and the two will become one flesh.' So they are no longer two, but one. Therefore what God has joined together, let man not separate" (Matthew 19:4-6).

Breaking the marriage covenant not only tears our one-flesh union apart but it tears apart our relationship with God, as well. We are told, "The Lord is acting as the witness between you and the wife of your youth, because you have broken faith with her, though she is your partner, the wife of your marriage covenant. Has not the Lord made them one? In flesh and spirit they are his ... So guard yourself in your spirit, and do not break faith with the wife of your youth" (Malachi 2:14-15).

Mom and Dad have remained faithful to each other through all the ups and downs, in sickness and in health, for 55 years. They would tell you it all comes down to faith. They have taken God at his word and when the going got tough, they remained faithful to

the covenant vows they made to each other before him. And he, in turn, faithfully gave them the grace to grow closer to each other and to him as they did for 55 years and counting.

I stopped in to visit my parents last week and Mom started telling me about all God had showed them that morning in their devotions, which they have done for most of theirs together. That, they would say, is the secret to their enduring marriage. You see, my parents have founded their lives upon God's word. And like the man who built his house on a solid foundation, "The rain came down, the streams rose, and the winds blew and beat against that house; yet it did not fall, because it had its foundation on the rock" (Matthew 7:25). There may have been times, over the years, where they might have thought, "We're all going to die," but the rock they built their lives and their marriage upon has remained firm.

Love remains faithful when it is founded on the Rock.

Faith Of Our Father

Hope.   — 1 Corinthians 13:13b

Jessie and Irving, as I mentioned in an earlier chapter, were married on September 19, 1948. I never had the privilege of meeting my father-in-law (thankfully, I know I will, someday) but sometimes I feel as though I already know him. From the time I met Bob and his family, I heard about the kind of man Irving C. Mondore had been, to all who had the blessing of knowing him. Of course, no one knew him as well as his three sons, his daughter, and most of all, his adoring wife, Jessie. I'm going to let Jessie tell you about him in her own words.

Those who knew Irving Mondore often commented about what a good, polite, intelligent, and honorable man he was. And yes, he was a kind, intelligent, generous, honest, and very likeable man. He was also a great husband and a very good father to his children. From early childhood, Irving was brought up by the golden rule: "Do unto others, as you would have them do unto you." Irv lived his entire life with that rule in his heart. One other thing he truly believed in was the Bible and a God who watches over us at all times. As a very young boy, his mother read to him from the Bible and then would explain it in her own words so he could understand it. His mother knew the Bible inside and out and lived by God's word. She was a schoolteacher and taught the golden rule to her schoolchildren. Life was hard back then but she and Irv's father did the best

they could to raise their five children but through it all, they never once lost their faith in God.

When Irv was a young boy at age thirteen or fourteen, his dad gave him a Bible and told him to "take time to read God's word as you go along in life, and as you go out into the world on your own." Irving did just that. He told me when we were talking of getting married that he had read the Bible through seven times and he learned more each time he did. Throughout his life, Irv kept God close to his heart. He was always saying, "Thanks, God" for this or that, or "if it wasn't for God, that wouldn't have happened." One day he received word that his dad was ill, too sick to continue running his farm back home. So Irv quit teaching and went home to run the farm for his dad. It wasn't long afterward that his dad died from pneumonia. Before he died, though, he took Irv's hand (he knew he was going to die) and he said, "Son, do not grieve, because we will be together again some day. Be happy and remember what I taught you. God is real." Irv never forgot that. He told that story to me many times and he believed it with all his heart.

When Irv and I got back together again after we broke up for two years, one of the first things he said to me was, "Here we are back seeing each other again. God wanted us to be together," and after I said I would marry him, he said, "Thank you, God."

Irv decided to make "You Are My Sunshine" our song. One night in later years, after the auction was over for the day, I kept waiting for him to come back to the house. At this point, Irving owned a large and successful auto auction. He was also struggling with cancer. I finally went back down to the auction and found him outside, just walking. Irv loved to walk. With every dealer now gone, he took my hand and said, "Let's just walk." He hadn't felt healthy for some time. We walked up to the back of the auction, opened up one of the cars, and sat in the front seat for some time. He held my hand and sang "our song" to me. He cried, and I cried, and he said, "I love you more than anything in this world." "I know, Irv. I love you, too." We both laughed. He then said, "You know I won't be here with you much longer," and I said, "We come into this world and we go out, right?" He kept quiet about anymore of that.

Some time later, Irv was very sick. He came home from the hospital for the last time and was here with us just two weeks. Nurses came to care for him during the daytime, and I cared for him at night and all through the weekend. He needed attention almost every hour on the hour. Before turning the light off each night, he always asked me to read the Bible to him. He knew exactly what he wanted me to read. Every night he asked me to read the same verses. I wrote them down and I still have the list.

> *For God so loved the world, that he gave his only begotten Son, that whosoever believeth in him should not perish, but have everlasting life.* — John 3:16

> *The heavens declare the glory of God; the skies proclaim the work of his hands.* — Psalm 19:1

> *Jesus said to her, "I am the resurrection and the life. He who believes in me will live, even though he dies."* — John 11:25

> *For this God is our God for ever and ever; he will be our guide even to the end.* — Psalm 48:14

> *Then make my joy complete, by being like-minded, having the same love, being one in spirit and purpose ... Each of you should look not only to your own interests, but also to the interests of others.* — Philippians 2:2, 4

> *It was revealed to them that they were not serving themselves but you, when they spoke of the things that have now been told you by those who have preached the gospel to you by the Holy Spirit sent from. Even angels long to look into these things. Therefore, prepare your minds for action; be self-controlled; set your hope fully on the grace to be given you when Jesus Christ is revealed. As obedient children, do not conform to the evil*

desires you had when you lived in ignorance. But just as he who called you is holy, so be holy in all you do; for it is written: "Be holy, because I am holy." Since you call on a Father who judges each man's work impartially, live your lives as strangers here in reverent fear. For you know that it was not with perishable things such as silver or gold that you were redeemed from the empty way of life handed down to you from your forefathers, but with the precious blood of Christ, a lamb without blemish or defect. — 1 Peter 1:12-19

One night after reading to him he said, "Put your hand on mine" (because he couldn't move his at all). So I did, and he looked into my eyes and he said very softly, "Jessie, you know I love the Lord, don't you?" I said, "Yes, Irv, I know you do." He said, "You know I'm going to leave you soon, don't you?" I said, "Yes, Irv." He said, "Don't you cry, Jessie. I want you to be brave for your sake and for the kids, and someday we will all be together again." He then said, "I'm not scared of dying, it's just the pain I don't like, but when I go, stand up and be brave, be kind to yourself and one day we will meet again." And one last thing he mentioned was, "I pray all things will be well with my family, and they will always be close." Two days later he had to go back to the hospital, and a short time later, Irving Mondore went home to be with the Lord.

Though not with us today, the legacy of this most wonderful man lives on. Everything Irv Mondore was and stood for, and all his fine good work he accomplished in the few short years he was here made a difference and left many precious memories with us all. I know in my heart he's with his dad and mom, and some day we all will be with him again. God be with you, Irv.

I am so thankful Jessie was willing to share these precious memories of her beloved Irving. They are a testimony of hope to all of us. Until the day the Lord returns, there will come a time in

every couple's lives when one partner must say good-bye to the other. But for every couple whose hope is in Christ, it is just a temporary interruption to a love that will be shared for eternity. As his favorite scriptures revealed, Irving had that absolute confidence as does Jessie who is eagerly anticipating their joyous reunion.

Love doesn't just hope to the end; it hopes to eternity.

There Is A River

And love.   — 1 Corinthians 13:13c

We hadn't been married all that long — maybe two months. We were up at my parents' camp in the Thousand Islands, sitting side-by-side on the dock, blissfully in love, and sharing what one could only describe as a perfect day. The sun was high in a deep blue sky filled with slowly meandering puffy clouds. The slight breeze stirred the water just enough to cause a delicate lapping sound against the shore and waft a scent of pine and fresh water our way. I looked across the wide Saint Lawrence River and was captivated by the splendor before me. "Could heaven really be any better than this?" I thought to myself. A silly question, I realize, but one I had asked myself before on a day such as today.

As we sat swinging our feet over the edge, Bob looked over just in time to see me start to cry. "What's wrong?" he asked with a worried look. I began to blurt out something about how we wouldn't be able to be married in heaven, pointing out where Jesus said, "At the resurrection people will neither marry nor be given in marriage; they will be like the angels in heaven" (Matthew 22:30), and that we would won't get to spend anymore time at our camp on the river together. Bob has long since given up trying to figure out what triggers these emotional outbursts. However, despite his confusion at the time, he was able to remind me of what we do know about heaven and how nothing we have in this life can compare to the glory that awaits us there.

I appreciated the reminder and quickly regained my composure. After all, I already knew what the Bible teaches about heaven. Jesus referred to it as paradise. Even as he hung on the cross, he

told the man dying next to him, "I tell you the truth, today you will be with me in paradise" (Luke 23:43). The apostle Paul was granted a glimpse of it in a vision and described it as being a place so extraordinary he had been forbidden to talk about it. He spoke of the experience as being "... caught up to paradise. He heard inexpressible things, things that man is not permitted to tell" (2 Corinthians 12:4). The Bible also tells us it is the marvelous reward given those who do not lose faith saying, "To him who overcomes, I will give the right to eat from the tree of life, which is in the paradise of God" (Revelation 2:7). That paradise is described as a place without sorrow or tears. We are assured that "there will be no more death or mourning or crying or pain, for the old order of things has passed away" (Revelation 21:4). It is also a place where we will be reunited with loved ones who died before us. The scriptures repeatedly speak of the death of a saint by saying he "was gathered to his people" (Genesis 35:29). But even as wonderful as that is, the ultimate joy of heaven will be in being eternally reunited with Jesus. This was the promise he gave his disciples before he left. He told them, "if I go and prepare a place for you, I will come back and take you to be with me that you also may be where I am" (John 14:3).

Later that evening, as I was having my devotions I came to a passage that I had previously marked in my Bible. This night, however, the words jumped out at me with new meaning, almost as if they were written in answer to my question: "God is our refuge and strength, an ever-present help in trouble. Therefore we will not fear, though the earth give way and the mountains fall into the heart of the sea ... There is a river whose streams make glad the city of God, the holy place where the most high dwells. God is within her, she will not fall; God will help her at break of day ..." (Psalm 46). My eyes became fixed on the words, "There is a river...." Familiar as they were, tonight they seemed to leap off the page as though I'd never seen them before. Whoever said God's heaven wouldn't have a river? Why, it made perfect sense that, if the river on this polluted and sin-soaked planet could be so stunningly beautiful, he would make a river far more lovely to adorn his own heavenly home. Would

the God who created this earth and said "It is good" not design a heaven — a paradise — of which he could say, "It is much better"?

I noticed a cross-reference I had marked in my Bible. I excitedly turned back just a few pages and read, "How priceless is your unfailing love! Both high and low among men find refuge in the shadow of your wings. They feast on the abundance of your house; you give them drink from your river of delights" (Psalm 36:7-8). Sure enough, there is a river awaiting me in heaven that the scriptures describe as a river of delights. Only the Creator, himself, could improve upon his already awesome and perfect work. So I suppose, I continued to reason, if the union to one person (like my beloved husband) could be so wonderful, imagine how much more wonderful it will be to be joined together with him, the rest of the body of Christ, and the Lord, himself, in heaven. In addition to the sheer joy of being one with him, this union would never end in sorrow or loss, but be eternal.

Our heavenly reunion will one day include parents, grandparents, family, friends, and all those who went on before us in Christ. In addition, it will ultimately include those we leave behind — children, grandchildren, and future generations we haven't even dreamed of. All who are his children will be eternally united as one with him and each other. What a glorious reunion it will be. The Bible uses the analogy of a physical body saying that "... we will in all things grow up into him who is the head, that is, Christ. From him the whole body, joined and held together by every supporting ligament, grows and builds itself up in love, as each part does its work" (Ephesians 4:15-16). This perfect love that we now have in Christ is what will bind us "... all together in perfect unity" (Colossians 3:14).

I finished reading the passages in the psalms and smiled as I put the Bible down. There is a river — a river of delights up there in heaven awaiting me. More importantly, whether I get there first, or he does, I will be able to share that river with my beloved Bob for eternity. Far beyond that, however, there is a Savior who loved both of us enough to prepare a place for us, and all the others who have trusted their lives to him so that we can be together with him.

As we walk together with him each day and grow in an eternal love relationship with him, we will, no doubt, find ourselves longing more and more for "the river whose streams make glad the city of God, the holy place where the most high dwells." It truly doesn't get any better than that.

**Love that glorifies God in this life together
will be even better in the next.**

Conclusion:
A Love Story*

But the greatest of these is love.

— 1 Corinthians 13:13d

Once upon a time, in a far away land, there was a great and mighty king. His kingdom was the greatest of kingdoms, beautiful and prosperous beyond imagination. The king had one son. He loved him very much. And the son loved his father. Since all of the kingdom would one day belong to his son, the king wanted his son to have a wife. Not just any wife, mind you, but the most beautiful bride in all of the world. So the king sent his servants throughout the earth to find the perfect bride for his son. They were to go everywhere, to every town or village in the kingdom until they found her. Off they went, to all of the farthest lands, to find a bride worthy of the king's son. At first, it seemed that none could be found. What were they to do? Then, finally, in one of the tiniest towns far from their glorious kingdom, they found her. She was everything the king's son could have ever longed for. She was more lovely than any other woman in the kingdom. Her dark eyes sparkled and seemed to dance with joy. She was sweet and gentle, loving and kind to all. She was the only child of a peasant couple and had spent her entire life caring for them, tending to their small flock of sheep. She had just reached the age where she could be courted. The servants observed all of this without revealing who they were. They returned home with great gladness.

When the servants reported what they had found to the king and his son, they were delighted. Indeed, there would soon be a glorious wedding — the wedding of the king's son. Or would there? The answer to this question could only be answered by the bride, herself. So, the king's son decided he would go to the far land where she lived and personally ask her to marry him. Surely she would be honored beyond words to be chosen by the king himself to be heir to all of his kingdom. Certainly no one could refuse such

an offer. However, the king was also very wise, and he realized the truth of these words. No one could refuse, but was that the kind of love relationship he wanted his beloved son to have with his bride? Wouldn't that make her more of a slave than a partner and wife? And if that was the case, wouldn't that be cheating his son out of the very thing he most wanted him to have? So the king came up with the perfect plan. He would send his son to the woman's land in a disguise. He would lay aside his robes and riches and put on the garments of a poor man. He would take on the role of a peasant in every way, living in the land and working to win the heart of his beautiful bride-to-be. If she would accept his offer of love and marriage, only then would he reveal himself to her in all his glory and take her to live with him as his bride in his father's kingdom.

And that is what he did. He came to the land where she lived, dressed in the most common of clothes, and got a menial job in her village. He did it all with one intent — to win her love. When the son first laid his eyes upon her, he was nearly overwhelmed by her beauty. She was everything he could have ever dreamed of. How he longed to take her as his wife. He immediately began to court her and at first she seemed smitten by his tender pursuits. But then things began to change. Many of the other men in the town had taken notice of her as well, and she of them. They offered her all kinds of riches (mind you, they were peasants), and made her all kinds of promises. Despite her growing love for the king's son, she was distracted by their lavish offers of wealth and prosperity and began to actively pursue them. The king's son was grieved when he saw what she was doing. He begged her to reconsider. She refused his loving gesture and turned, instead, to the lovers who sought her affections. But instead of giving her the love they had promised, they began to abuse her, and beat her, and to take away the little she and her family had. Soon she was left, bruised and beaten, with nothing. She was too ashamed to go back to the king's son. Surely he would no longer want her, now damaged goods, after having so blatantly betrayed and rejected him.

The maiden didn't really understand how deeply the king's son loved her. Even when she was unable to even cry out for his help, he knew what was happening (he had been keeping a watchful eye on her all along — he had never stopped loving her). As a gang of her former lovers approached her to do her more harm, the king's son suddenly appeared. Even knowing his own life would be in danger, he came to her rescue with only one thought in mind — he must save his beloved. As expected, the whole mob of wicked men turned on him and began beating him with wooden clubs. He fell to the ground, bleeding and broken, and with his last gasp before losing consciousness, he looked up at the maiden and said, "I've never stopped loving you."

Her heart was broken and she burst into tears. She ran toward him as he fell. "I'm so sorry. Please forgive me. I still love you, too and I need you ..." but before she reached him, the men grabbed her and carried her away into the darkness. She realized that, because of her own unfaithfulness, everything she had ever hoped for was gone. It no longer mattered to her what they would do to her. Without her beloved, what was there to live for? As the men surrounded her and began to move closer, in her utter despair she cried out, knowing there was no one to hear her — no one to come and rescue her.

Then, suddenly, appearing from out of nowhere, he came. The king's son stood before her, this time not dressed as a peasant but in full royal armor and surrounded with the king's soldiers. The maiden cried out in joyous unbelief. "I thought you were dead." The evil mob scattered into the night with the king's army in hot pursuit. Soon, it was only the king's son and the tattered but beautiful maiden standing together in the moonlight. He reached over and brushed a spot of dirt off her cheek. "Will you marry me? Will you come away with me to my father's kingdom and be my bride?" The maiden took only a few moments to recover from the shock of realizing the truth about who her beloved really was. All she cared about at that moment was that he was alive and that, despite all she had done, he still loved her enough to come and rescue her. She fell on her knees before him and said, "Will you forgive me for ever

doubting your love?" She grabbed his hand, the hand of one who had worked like peasant to win her love, and she kissed it adoringly. "There is no one I would rather be in all of the universe than your wife." And they lived happily ever after. By the way, you're all invited to the wedding!

> *I saw the Holy City, the new Jerusalem, coming down out of heaven from God, prepared as a bride beautifully dressed for her husband. And I heard a loud voice from the throne saying, "Now the dwelling of God is with men, and he will live with them. They will be his people, and God himself will be with them and be their God. He will wipe every tear from their eyes. There will be no more death or mourning or crying or pain, for the old order of things has passed away." He who was seated on the throne said, "I am making everything new!" ... The Spirit and the bride say, "Come!" And let him who hears say, "Come!" Whoever is thirsty, let him come; and whoever wishes, let him take the free gift of the water of life.*   — Revelation 21:2-5; 22:17

The End

* Adapted from "The Parable of the King and the Maiden" by Soren Kierkegaard in *Philosophical Fragments* (Johannes Climacus, ed. Sören Kierkegaard, 1844). http://www.religion-online.org/showchapter.asp?title=2512&C=2380.